HEREDITY AND HUMAN LIFE

Heredity and Human Life

HAMPTON L. CARSON

Columbia University Press, New York and London

COPYRIGHT © 1963 COLUMBIA UNIVERSITY PRESS

ISBN 0-231-02551-3 *Clothbound*
ISBN 0-231-08558-3 *Paperback*

PRINTED IN THE UNITED STATES OF AMERICA

9 8 7 6 5 4

To Meredith

PREFACE

REVOLUTIONARY advance in science in this century is connected in the popular mind with spectacular accomplishments in atomic energy, space engineering, and the control of disease. Simultaneously, however, but almost unnoticed, basic biological science has had a revolution of its own. New information now exists which enables us to probe the deepest scientific question the human mind can raise: the nature and the origin of life and man. These new scientific realities provide the most powerful tool ever available for understanding ourselves as individuals and in our relationship to our fellow human beings.

Biology is the science of life. There should not be any confusion of biology with pathology, which is a kind of biological engineering in which the medical man is charged with the job of healing the sick. Although not yet won universally, the physician's battle against ignorance and superstition has made impressive gains. The achievements of medicine and the alleviation of human suffering that it has brought speak a universal language which reaches into every culture. But who speaks for the well man? Who takes the long view of the human species, of its origin and fate? This is the proper role for the fundamental biologist who, like the physicist and chemist, continues to probe the deeper questions which lie behind the extraordinary accomplishments of modern engineering.

The purpose of this book is to set down the key facts about

human biology, especially concerning human origins and human heredity, in as direct and simple a manner as possible. The only editorial tone is the insistence that these facts be known and weighed by every person who wants to cultivate a rational approach to himself and to the broader problems of human relationships and welfare.

Scientific facts such as these presented here do not of themselves lead to any obvious program of personal morals or social or political action. They embody no automatic guarantees of security. But there is no excuse for any rational action taken in ignorance of them. Irrational actions, especially in the human relations field, arise partly out of ignorance but mostly from emotional reactions like fear. Understanding an attribute or a person blunts and deters this irrational fear. Thus, dissemination of the bare facts themselves may help begin to alleviate some of the awful consequences of fear, the psychological inturn that comes out first as prejudice and bigotry, then as hate, and finally as open conflict.

Ignorance of the nature of man has historically provided the most fertile ground for bigotry. The main food which sustained Hitlerism was the continued use of racist nonsense. Pseudoscience blunted the reason of millions of intelligent people while millions more looked on, hardly believing that it could be happening. Let us not be apathetic to the fact that racist nonsense has been, and continues to be, the biggest psychological excuse for man's inhumanity to man.

Each generation of men has left its mark on human thought and action. Ours promises to be the age in which the intelligence and reason of the scientific attitude will reach deeply into human affairs. If this promise is to be realized, vague and mystical doctrines of all sorts must give way to rational ones. We cannot exist half mystic and half scientific. The scientific approach and any success it may have in guiding human affairs requires a life-

PREFACE

time of training in separating fact from fancy, realities from self-deceit. This attitude must reach into every corner of our lives. The great majority of children in the world, for example, receive religious instruction which presents a vague and mystical account of the origin and nature of man. Does this aid the development of the critical faculties which are so desperately needed for rational solution of the problems of the modern world?

Biological facts touch every individual so closely and personally that many persons are afraid that if they look too closely they will find something basically fearful, something about themselves or others which might deny human aspirations or dignity. Rather than holding such new terrors, scientific knowledge of man provides a basis for dispelling them.

This book recounts the origin of the individual from special cells of his parents. These cells contain a combination of chemical determiners, the genes, which automatically build a detailed framework on which life experience finally constructs the individuality of the person. Except for certain kinds of twins, no two persons begin with identical biological inheritances. This means that each one of us, past, present, and future, is unique. This uniqueness is further accentuated by the circumstance that no two persons have the same set of experiences. Both heredity and environment are partners in shaping the personality and both have a great effect on important characters.

Man is then considered as a species, as a group which is a part of nature. Like the rest of current living things, man has evolved from humbler beginnings. Rather than degrading him, this fact dignifies him and renders him all the more remarkable. After looking at the historical record, the mode of human evolution as a process is examined. The origin and evolution of man was recent and rapid. The small size and clanlike structure of these early populations seems to have been their most important feature. Existing human races were formed when the new human species spread over the world from its ancestral home, which was probably Africa. Races are geographical and genetic subdivisions of mankind; they were formed very late in history indeed, at a time after the full power of the human brain had evolved. In view of this, the fact that there is no evidence of genetic inferiority in mental capacity of any group is understandable. Despite profound differences wrought by isolation, language, and custom, men have a common mental heritage. Individual variation in the genetic basis of mental capacity, nevertheless, universally occurs within each human group.

Writing an account such as this is an unfamiliar and difficult assignment for a scientist. The approach is intended to be nontechnical. When an attempt to "popularize" a scientific subject is made, there inevitably results a vagueness that to some extent defeats the very purpose of the popular treatment. This problem has led many scientists to declare that communication of the kind I am attempting here is unfruitful and represents a disservice to the profession.

I cling to the view that there is a distinction between picking out and explaining the essence of a discovery and a full technical understanding of it. To say that the earth is round rather than flat is to abstract a basic scientific finding in a simple and correct manner. The further technicality that on close scrutiny the earth is not a perfect sphere does not affect the truth, in essence, of the first statement.

Accordingly, I ask indulgence in this venture from those with serious interest and competence in biology. Beyond the beginning student in biology, who may wish to look here for a measure of orientation to the larger view, this book will offer little of value to the professional biologist, except perhaps that the crudities of this attempt might stimulate more successful efforts.

PREFACE

The book is designed to be most useful for teachers, social workers, and ministers, without regard to particular religious affiliation, who deal with people and their problems on a daily basis. They owe it to themselves and to those that they influence to be informed.

"Taking biology in school" is not enough for the citizen of the modern world. It is not enough to collect and press leaves, memorize the names of the song birds, and learn a little about animal reproduction. The great philosophical core of biology is not to be grasped by dilute nature study, anatomy, or hygiene. The essentials must be seen directly and keenly.

This book deals mostly with the human individual as a biological entity and explores his relationship to his immediate family, his ancestors, and the broader segment of humanity of which he is a part. It is certainly more dignified and more usual to circumlocute, using the third person singular, so that the reader may have the privilege of excluding himself as exemplary material if he so wishes. In dealing with human genetics, however, one must continually treat individuals, their mates, their reproduction, and their reproductive cells. It seems discursively very wasteful to turn things around into the third person when you, the reader, can serve as the clearest embodiment of what is being talked about. Accordingly, I hope that the reader will not be annoyed by being frequently addressed in the second person. If I were a chemist, physicist, or geologist, writing about my science, then no justification for so addressing the reader could be found.

The bulk of this book was written as an extracurricular activity when I was at the University of Melbourne, Australia on a Fulbright Fellowship. I wish to thank Professor M. J. D. White of the Department of Zoology for his hospitality and his forbearance. Responsibility for the book and any faults it may have is mine but it is a pleasure to acknowledge the inspiration and continual encouragement of Professor Th. Dobzhansky. My wife, Meredith Shelton Carson, not only prepared the index but made many valuable suggestions all along the way.

St. Louis, Missouri
July, 1962
HAMPTON L. CARSON

CONTENTS

	Preface	vii
1.	Origin of the Individual	1
2.	The Hereditary Information	14
3.	Stability of the Hereditary Material	31
4.	Combinations and Recombinations of Genes	57
5.	Heredity and Environment	74
6.	The Individual and His Group	100
7.	Origin of the Human Species	118
8.	Evolutionary Forces As Applied to Man	135
9.	Isolation and Race Formation	150
10.	The Historic Breakdown of Isolation	166
11.	Heredity and Human Understanding	179
	Notes	199
	General References	211
	Index	215

FIGURES

1. Human egg and sperm, photographed in the living state   *following page* 12
2. The human embryo
3. A dividing human cell
4. Chromosomes of a normal man
5. Inheritance of coat color in the guinea pig   17
6. Mating of two black guinea pigs, each of which is a carrier of the gene for white   19
7. Chromosomes of a human male arranged so as to show the existence of pairs   22
8. Sex determination in man   23
9. Occurrence and inheritance of a dominant mutation in man   33
10. Radiation damage to a human cell   37
11. Chromosome group of an individual human male   58
12. Comparison of mitosis and meiosis   60
13. Recombination at meiosis   67
14. Average differences between one-egg twins compared with those between like-sexed two-egg twins   84
15. Likeness of one-egg twin pairs compared with two-egg twin pairs, for cases where at least one member shows the trait   86
16. Heredity and environment in mental accomplishment   93
17. Maximum number of ancestors in six generations   102

18. "Loss of ancestors" due to relationship between some of them   103
19. The founding and growth of a population with tendencies towards inbreeding and isolation   105
20. Population founding under conditions where the gene pool remains single with moderate outbreeding   115
21. Time scale of the last 25 million years of earth history, together with an interpretative diagram of the evolution of apelike and manlike forms   123
22. Time scale of the last million years of earth history, the Pleistocene   128

HEREDITY AND HUMAN LIFE

Chapter 1

ORIGIN OF THE INDIVIDUAL

Fertilized egg

SOMEWHAT less than a century ago, the discovery was made that every human individual begins as a separate bit of living matter produced by his parents. This bit, the fertilized egg, contains within itself all the information necessary for the development of the complicated adult body, a smooth-functioning whole, complete in all its parts.

The facts of the immediate origin of the individual rank among the most sensational discoveries of modern science. Development from a minute informational speck to a complex but specific form is a rule of life in all living things. Stated in a slightly different way, we may say that life continually renews itself by making new individuals, but the origin of these is always from pre-existing life of a closely similar sort.

Behind you and me in history, then, lies a stream of individuals who, although they were mortal, nevertheless have a degree of immortality in the very existence of ourselves, just as we will have immortality in our descendants. Being alive, and thus being a carrier of this information, is quite literally a hereditary trust bequeathed to each individual from millions of individuals who lived in past generations. Our connection to them through the hereditary material is not vague or nebulous; it is a concrete scientific reality. A living being is not a temporary phantom, living and dying in isolation. Its informational system confers on it an historical character which bridges back into the remote past, generation over generation.

Since this discovery, we have been trying to answer the further question of just how so small a bit of substance can contain so much information. The fertilized egg produces an individual whose characteristics reflect past biological history, but, even beyond this, it contains instructions which confer on each new individual that absolute uniqueness which each person has. We want also to find out how this information is able to express itself, to make its influence felt and to guide development along the precise path called for in its particular hereditary line.

Cell and nucleus

Going just a little back in the history of a fertilized egg, we now know that it, in turn, arises from the coming together of two quite separate bits of living substance, the egg and the sperm. These two objects have been recognized, again for about a hundred years, as being quite comparable, at least in size and contents, to the other cells which comprise the adult body. The unit called the cell is a very small mass of living substance enclosed within a fine filmlike membrane. This membrane is very delicate; if it is broken, the living substance itself will ooze out. Free from the confines of the cell, it loses its unique property of being alive and dies immediately.

Near the center of the cell is a special area which is separated from the rest of the living substance by another membrane, similar in delicacy to the one which is on the outside of the whole cell. This central structure is the cell nucleus. It contains a special chemical substance with an extremely complicated structure, as shown by studies from the microscopical, chemical, and physical points of view. The material inside the nucleus has properties which stagger the imagination and challenge our powers to contemplate it. In this century we have found that the information lies here, quite literally in the form of a complex and detailed code. An entire modern science—genetics—has been built up around the properties of this coded biological material of the cell nucleus.

Both egg and sperm are very small. The approximate size of the human egg can be visualized in the following way. Pull out a hair and let it fall on a piece of white paper. The diameter of the egg is close to the diameter of this hair; this means you have to visualize a section of the hair cut off so that it is not any longer than wide. The nucleus is even smaller, about one-fifth the diameter of the whole egg (Fig. 1).

Complexity in small-sized objects need no longer surprise us. The living world of microorganisms, from which we were locked out until the discovery of the microscope, is a gross one when compared with that of the atomic and molecular events which we can now observe with our present scientific devices. Modern instrumentation has long since left the stage wherein the normal human senses are merely augmented; many of these machines are indeed themselves new senses, able to detect events which were previously utterly beyond our reach. They are designed to translate their findings into something having direct meaning for us. The living state is admittedly more difficult to investigate than the nonliving because the condition of being alive is so easily destroyed. Nevertheless, new methods have made possible extraordinarily detailed analyses of the structure and function of the smallest particles of hereditary material.

Material nature of living substance

Living matter does not differ from nonliving because it has within it some elusive, nonmaterial vital principle. But this idea of a special "life-substance" has died a very slow death. There is no real evidence for the existence of such a "force," but the idea has hung on because of the general feeling of incredulity that biological material could be so complex at the molecular level. Living things can do so many extraordinary things when compared to nonliving material that it has been hard to accept them as another part of the physical world. Nevertheless, a great weight of modern research has provided abundant evidence that there is indeed no magic genie within the cell. We find there only atoms and molecules of a sort no different, except in complexity, from those found in nonliving things. Many of the chemical substances present are commonplace ones which have been drawn unchanged from the inorganic world outside the cell membrane. But other substances, formed within the cell, show a complexity in structure and function unknown in nonliving substances. It is these substances, mostly complex proteins, that give life its uniqueness.

Origin of species and origin of life

The facts about the origin of the individual clarify the role of two other kinds of biological origin. With respect to man, discussion of the origin of the species group to which he belongs will be deferred to a later chapter. Briefly, though, we may say that descent, in most types of living things, is accompanied by stepwise, slight but permanent changes in heredity. This evolutionary process, extending over millions of generations, alters the code in the fertilized eggs and can account for the present diversity of animals and plants. The way evolution works, however, is a separate problem from the origin of life in the first place.

There is general agreement that life originated under conditions which existed on the earth a billion years or more ago. These conditions no longer exist, so that we cannot hope to observe the origination process occurring naturally at the present time.[1] Despite this, extraordinary progress has recently been made towards the creation of laboratory conditions wherein certain of the basic events fundamental to the origin of life may be studied. In the first place, it is clear that a period of chemical evolution in the primeval seas, especially of carbon-containing compounds, must have been a necessary condition prior to the emergence of the living state. That simple proteins could arise naturally within mixtures of such compounds has been experimentally demonstrated.[2] The big step from this point seems to be the origin of some kind of organization within these primordial substances. This has been visualized as having its beginning in various droplets or lumps of material suspended in a watery matrix, much like a thin organic soup. Various very slow chemical reactions, involving at first simple and later more complex carbon-containing compounds, might be expected to proceed under these conditions in such droplets. Life as we know it, however, could be said to have arisen only when these chemical reactions had become regularized and speeded up and when the capacity to carry them out was somehow rendered permanent and transmissible.

In only very recent years, the matter of the origin of life has become a subject of serious laboratory study. It seems likely that it will be possible in the near future to put together artificially a self-reproducing physico-chemical system which can sustain itself if given an energy source. If this is indeed done, it would amount to an artificial synthesis of the living process in its most basic properties.

Egg, sperm, and the hereditary process

The egg and sperm are not exceptional cells; their physics and chemistry differ in no fundamental way from any other living matter. Most people learn to associate the word egg with that of the chicken or perhaps the less grandiose but nevertheless relatively very large eggs of fish or aquarium snails. Mere large size of these types of eggs does not, in itself, make them very different from extremely small ones like the human egg or that of a dog or cat. The size difference in eggs from one sort of life to another is mostly due to the fact that they have differing amounts of stored food material. Yolk is nothing more than stored food which serves as an immediately available source of energy for the new growing individual. Yolk is not living substance; it is rather the first staff of life. It is used by the stuff of life, the living substance itself, as a source of energy from which the living material is able to maintain itself and make more of itself.

If we had some special solvent which would dissolve away only yolk, and if we applied it to different kinds of eggs, it is quite likely that the real amount of living material left in the case of bird, fish, and human would be about the same. Human eggs, like those of other mammals, dry out almost instantly if exposed to air. They must always be surrounded by fluid if they are to survive. Other superficial differences between eggs are due to the presence, in some cases, of protective egg shells or jelly coats.

Except in unusual circumstances,[3] an egg alone is not sufficient to start an individual of the next generation. Fertilization by a sperm must occur first. An egg is said to have been fertilized when it has been approached by a sperm and has subsequently actually taken this sperm in through its outer membrane. The sperm is clearly a cell but an unusual one because it consists almost entirely of the same general type of substance found in the nucleus of the egg cell and, for that matter, in all other nuclei. This makes up what is called the "head" of the cell. The rest of the cell takes the form of a long motile tail. In a very real sense the sperm is almost all nucleus, that is, pure hereditary material.

Its contents and properties are nearly identical to that of the egg nucleus, thus explaining the equal potency of the two parents in inheritance.[4]

The paradox in inheritance: like produces likenesses which are not exact

Biological inheritance can be paraphrased as "like produces like," but we must be careful not to think of this in extremely specific terms. When we say that the "offspring resemble the parents" we mean to imply a general resemblance, rather than identity with the parents in a detailed and strict sense, down to the last molecule.

Consider the following example. If you have a female cat as a pet, she is likely to produce kittens, with the father probably unknown to you. Now, when the kittens come, there is no difficulty in seeing the first basic fact of heredity: the fertilized eggs have produced kittens and kittens only. The second fact about the litter is not so immediately self-evident. Examined closely, none of these kittens is an exact replica of the mother. Suppose she is a tortoise-shell tabby (yellow spots on a gray striped background): some of the kittens may be wholly black or wholly yellow; some might be a very light washed-out blue (maltese). In others, there might be areas of white not present in the mother.

If there are some female kittens which are tortoise-shell tabbies like their mother, the yellow spots will very probably not be in the same place or of the same size. Like has produced like, but the likeness does not result in exact replicates. Herein lies the paradoxical and confusing dilemma that the student of heredity faces. He must explain on the one hand how the general biological similarities (that is, "catness," in our example) are maintained from generation to generation, and at the same time he must provide an explanation of how relatively minor variations on this general theme arise.

Hereditary determinants in the fertilized egg and their later expression in the individual

Knowledge of certain other facts is basic to the understanding of the nature of inheritance. We do not inherit characters themselves, we inherit determinants for characters. These determinants, in some instances, dictate very precisely the details of characters, although the degree of determination varies within limits which we will examine later. Suffice it to say here that determination commonly extends to a very great variety of final features. In man, for instance, some of these, like hair texture and color, eye color, shape of facial features, and body build are easily observed. Specific determination commonly also extends to less easily observed but perhaps more important things, such as the blood serotypes and certain features of the mental apparatus.

When we speak of heredity, we tend to think in terms of a strong and highly deterministic force. This determinism, however, is by no means absolute. For a preliminary series of simple examples, consider the following. Hair structure is strongly affected by hereditary determinants already present in the fertilized egg. These determinants may call for straight hair. If so, the hair of the individual will be straight as it grows from the hair follicle. Thereafter, however, it is subject to change if one applies a strong environmental directive agent, such as a curling iron. A certain determinant may be present in the fertilized egg which results, after development into an adult, in a subnormal pancreas, one which makes insufficient insulin. If intake of sugar is high, the condition known as diabetes may result. If intake of sugar is low, the disease may never develop at all. In any case, development of the disease may be controlled by medical administration of insulin, thus artificially supplying the substance for which the hereditary information was imperfect.

Understanding the interplay between hereditary determinants and environmental influences on characters is a key area in genetics. Many people have the notion that if a character is affected by an hereditary determinant it is somehow unchangeable just because of this fact. The above examples show that this is not so. In short, it may be said that the result depends on what particular character you are talking about; some can be easily changed and others cannot. Understanding the interplay between hereditary and environmental determinants on the final expression of a character has been one of the crowning achievements of modern genetics. A further discussion is found in Chapter 5.

Growth, cell division, and cell differences

How can a determinant within the nucleus of a fertilized egg ultimately make its effect felt, for example, in the form of the hair as it grows from the hair follicles in the adult person? This is one of the major unsolved problems of biology but some facts help us to make an approach to an answer.

The adult differs from the fertilized egg which gave rise to it in three ways. First, it is larger. The living substance found within the egg has the property of growth, that is, of manufacturing more of its own substance. Second, the growth is accompanied by the increase in the number of cells from one to many millions. Actually, we know now that a cell grows principally by taking in through its membrane various raw materials which it builds, by complex chemical synthesis, into more living substance like itself. In the process, the cell gets larger and heavier. Since the combustion and synthesis and other molecular events that take place within the cell work best in a unit of small size, growth is followed, at least ordinarily, by what is called cell division; thus cell division in most cases reflects the fact that growth has occurred.

Finally, let us consider the third way that the adult differs from the fertilized egg. It is not merely a collection of cells each of which is identical in structure to the beginning cell. Groups of cells have become different in structure and function, forming what we recognize as muscle, brain, skin, or hair cells (Fig. 2). From the point of view of heredity, furthermore, it is important to note that in one part of the body (the testis in males and the ovary in females) cells capable of starting the whole process over again are produced.

Nuclear division and the chromosomes

When a cell divides, and is watched in the living condition, it undergoes a series of changes of shape; it can be seen to go from spherical to elliptical, then to a dumbbell form, finally it pulls apart completely into two separate units (Fig. 3). When this happens, the nucleus inside also regularly divides into two, but the details are hard to see in the living specimen. Methods of aiding visibility by staining the contents of cells with dyes go back to the nineteenth century and have now been refined to a point such that we know in quite minute detail what goes on as a cell divides.

As the nucleus is the seat of the hereditary factors in all cells, what happens within it during division is of particular interest. When a cell is dividing, however, a remarkable cycle of changes occurs within the nucleus. What was prior to division a seemingly rather vague and formless material which stains dark with certain dyes, now resolves itself into a definite and predictable number of rod-, J-, or V-shaped units, the chromosomes. Under high magnification and in conditions when the chromosomes are in their most shortened state, each can be recognized as an individually separate element (Fig. 4).

In a normal human cell, and in the fertilized egg as well, 46 chromosomes may be counted as the nucleus prepares to divide. Close inspection of these shows that each chromosome is composed of two halves. Following a precise series of movements, which go off with an extraordinary precision, the two halves of each chromosome split apart and one of the halves goes into each of the two products of the dividing nucleus.

The result is very simple: each daughter cell produced from the splitting of one mother cell gets a complete longitudinal replica of each of the 46 chromosomes. Thus, the two nuclei which result are exactly equivalent in the hereditary material that each gets from the original nucleus. Each gets an exact copy of the original and from this copy builds another double set.

Nuclear sameness within the individual

This process of nuclear division, therefore, is the major mechanism which maintains sameness in the hereditary material. In this process, like produces like on a cellular, chromosome, and, indeed, in this case, molecular level. It is important to note that this mode of nuclear division, mitosis, normally produces exact duplications only; this process is the principal adaptation of life to the maintenance of exact hereditary continuity.

Just at the beginning of development, when the growing individual consists of only two cells, an occasional rare accident may occur so that these two become separated from one another. Instead of staying together and eventually producing the one mass of millions of cells that we recognize as an adult, both of these replicates of one fertilized egg may develop side by side within the mother. The result is the production of identical twins, the exception to the rule that each individual starts from a different and hereditarily unique fertilized egg.

Ordinarily, however, the cells stay together in one embryonic unit and the multiplication of cells, each with its nucleus, proceeds. All resulting cells retain this same hereditary content, thus the evidence is overwhelming that the cells of your fingers and toes, blood, bone, and brain contain that precise set of determiners that was originally present in the fertilized egg from which you began.

Molecular differences between individuals

Most of the facts given above have not only been gleaned by the study of the human, but have been verified by studying many other kinds of living things as well. They are facts which are revealed mostly by fairly simple methods of microscopic examination of cells. Even by these methods, the chromosomes reveal themselves as structures of remarkable constancy and precision; however, a number of questions remain. In the first place, if we examine the chromosomes of persons of obviously widely different heredity, for example, persons of Scandinavian, African, or Asiatic origin, they appear to be exactly the same, as far as our observations are able to go. Yet our analysis of the nature of the hereditary information, which will be approached shortly in the next chapter, reveals that there are many real hereditary differences between the fertilized eggs of not only such different individuals but even between such closely related individuals as brothers in the same family. What does this mean? It means that the differences we are looking for must be beyond the easy reach of the microscope. The differences between the chromosomes of such individuals must be at the molecular or at least the submicroscopic level. To go further in this direction, we must employ different methods; using the microscope does not give us all the information we need.

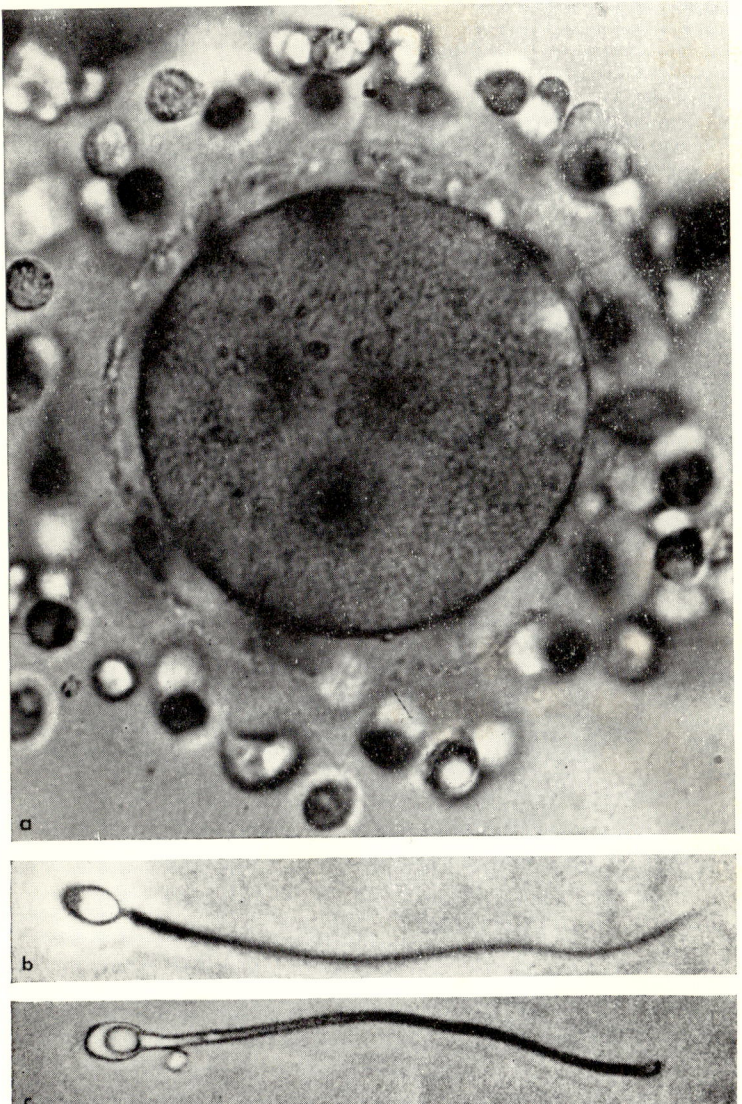

Fig. 1. Human egg and sperm, photographed in the living state

(a) An ovum; it has a number of smaller cells, seen as dark and light objects, adhering to its surface, which shows as a dark circle. Magnified 480 times. Photograph courtesy of Professor W. J. Hamilton. (b), (c) Sperm cell showing head and tail, photographed at different focal levels. The small circle within the head in (c) is the nucleus. Magnified 2140 times. Photographs courtesy of C. van Duijn, Jr.

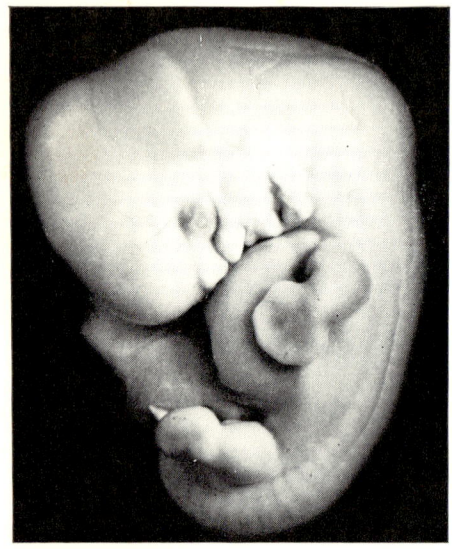

Fig. 2.
The human embryo

(a) Photograph of an embryo at approximately 35 days of gestation. The facial features are not complete; the arms and legs can be seen as padlike extensions. A tail, which is later absorbed, can also be seen. About six times natural size.

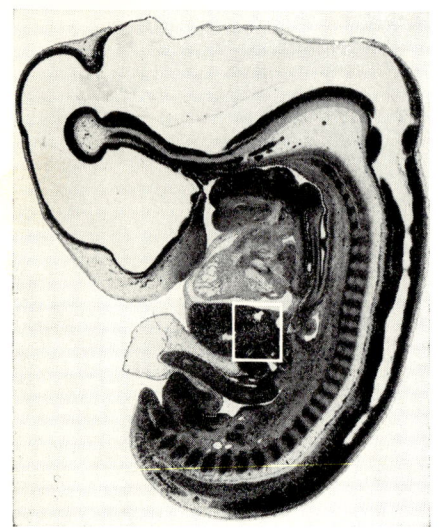

(b) A stained slice from the same embryo. The backbone can be seen extending down into the tail. The brain area is very large. The section within the rectangle shows a portion of the liver and intestine.

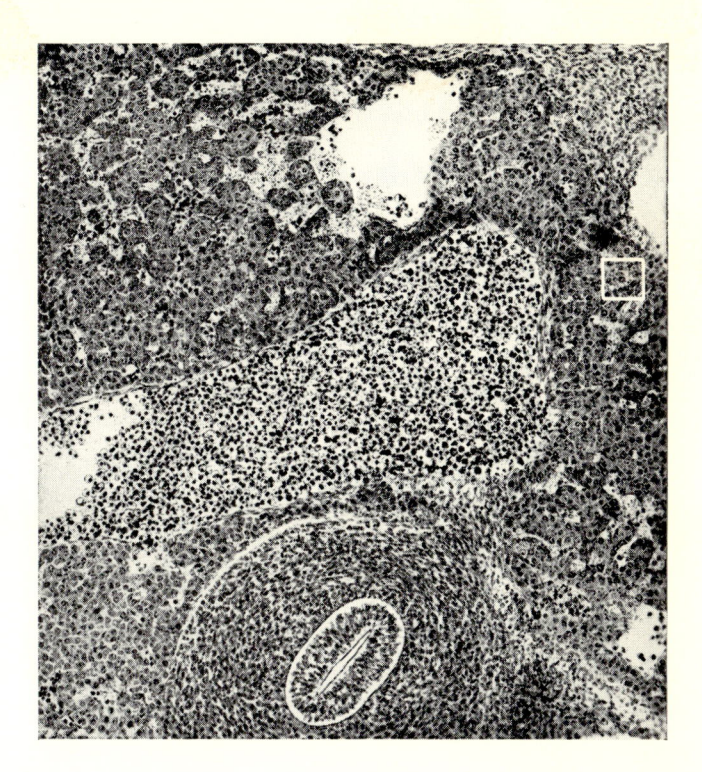

(c) A detailed view of the section within the rectangle in (b). The dark spots throughout the section are the nuclei containing the hereditary information of each cell. Magnified about 100 times.

(d) A drawing of four liver cells from the enclosed square section in (c). The outline of each cell is shown with the dark, spherical nucleus in the center. Magnified about 2150 times. (a), (b), and (c) Courtesy of Dr. Mary E. Rawles.

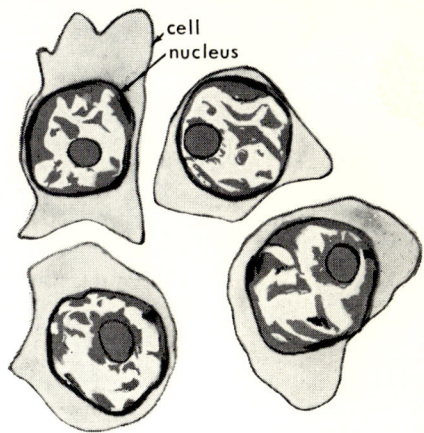

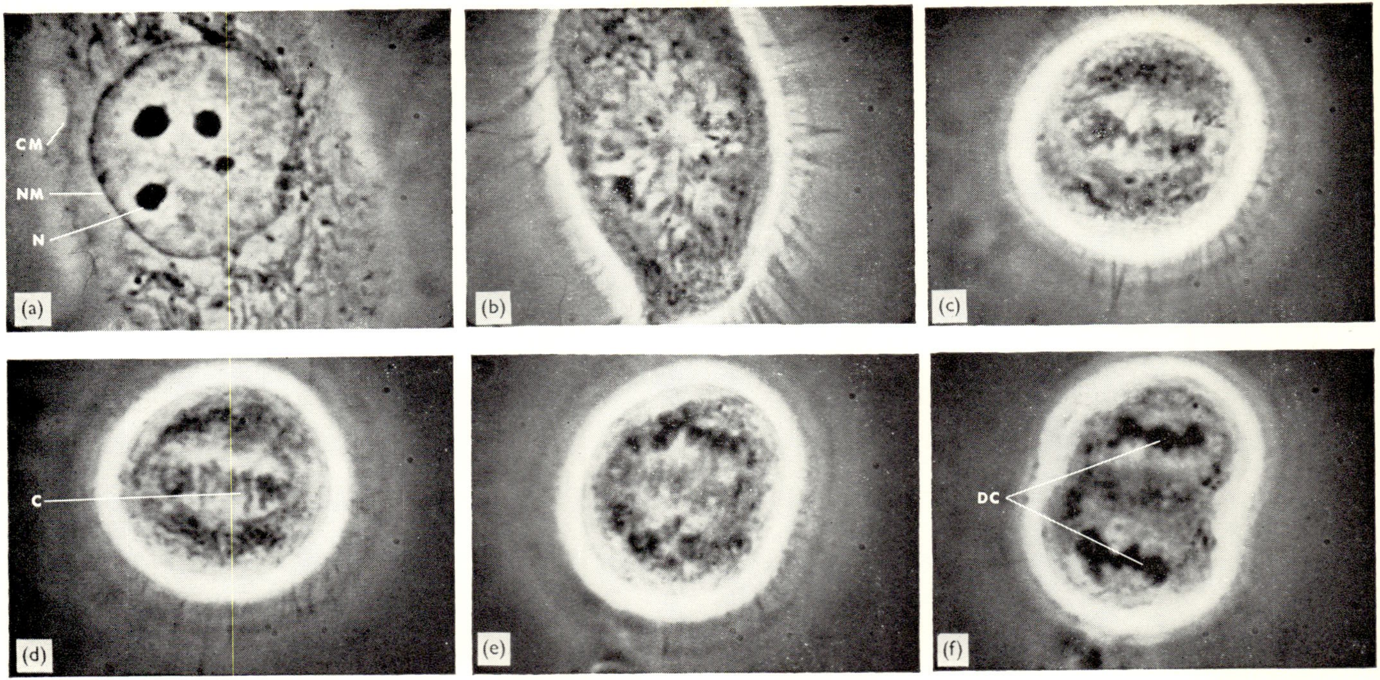
CM
NM
N
(a)
(b)
(c)
C
(d)
(e)
DC
(f)

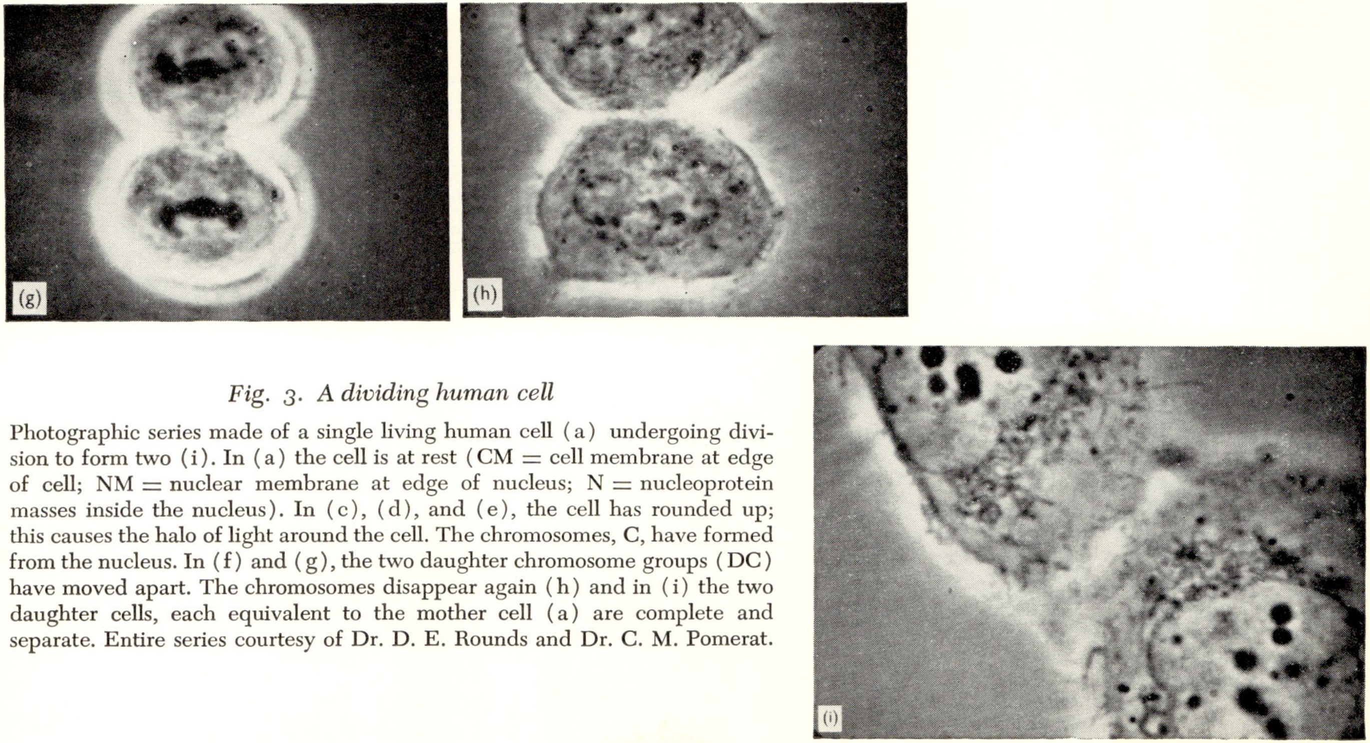

Fig. 3. A dividing human cell

Photographic series made of a single living human cell (a) undergoing division to form two (i). In (a) the cell is at rest (CM = cell membrane at edge of cell; NM = nuclear membrane at edge of nucleus; N = nucleoprotein masses inside the nucleus). In (c), (d), and (e), the cell has rounded up; this causes the halo of light around the cell. The chromosomes, C, have formed from the nucleus. In (f) and (g), the two daughter chromosome groups (DC) have moved apart. The chromosomes disappear again (h) and in (i) the two daughter cells, each equivalent to the mother cell (a) are complete and separate. Entire series courtesy of Dr. D. E. Rounds and Dr. C. M. Pomerat.

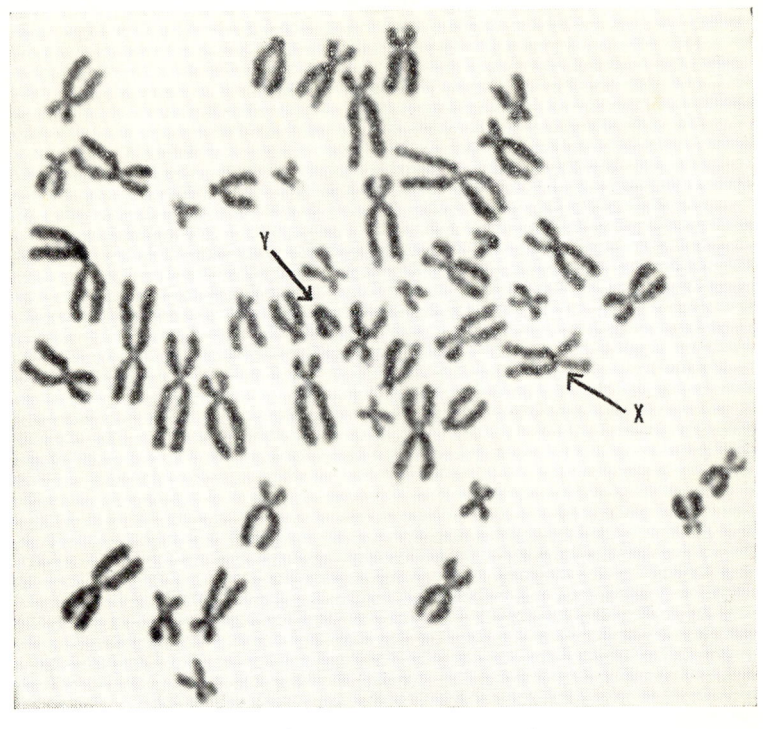

Fig. 4. Chromosomes of a normal man

While it was dividing, this cell was treated so that the chromosomes were shortened and spread out and rendered more visible by staining with a dye. In the resulting photograph of the dead cell, the full normal number of 46 chromosomes is visible. Each appears split down its length; the two halves are held together at only one point, so that each chromosome resembles an "X." If the cell had been allowed to divide, one longitudinal half of each chromosome (the left or right half of the X) would have gone into each daughter cell. The chromosomes labeled X and Y are the sex chromosome pair characteristic of the male. These will be discussed in Chapter 2. Figure courtesy of Dr. J. H. Tjio.

Summary

Each person and other living thing which has male and female parents begins as a minute bit of living matter, the fertilized egg. This original cell has the capacity to burn food for energy and to utilize and build itself up with other raw materials. In so doing, it performs a feat unique to living things: it grows, one cell giving rise to millions. During this process it makes more of its own specific substance and comes to resemble its parents closely, but does not show identity to either of them. What it inherits is a pattern, or code, by which development is controlled. The pattern has been handed down, with slight changes, over uncounted generations.

Within the single cell which we are at our own beginning is a nucleus which contains an informational recording of our respective biological pasts; this is in the form of 46 long threadlike structures, the chromosomes. When the fertilized egg, or any of its descendants, divides, each of these 46 elements likewise divides exactly and then duplicates itself so that each daughter cell gets a complete set. Whatever biological inheritance you receive from your parents, and through them from your whole biological past, must come across the narrow hereditary bridge associated with these chromosomes. The fact that the chromosome sets of different normal persons of like sex of the human species are identical to microscopical examination reflects the biological kinship of all men. Hereditary differences between people, such as eye color, skin color, hair structure, and blood chemistry, result from submicroscopic differences in the chromosomes, most of which are at the molecular level. Differences of this sort are often quite striking, even between children of the same parents. Only identical, or one-egg, twins appear to begin with precisely the same informational code on the chromosomes.

Chapter 2

THE HEREDITARY INFORMATION

The gene

HEREDITY involves the transferring of some sort of information from one generation to the next. This fact has been strongly indicated for almost as long as controlled breeding of animals and plants has been practiced. Consider a simple example from the breeding of guinea pigs. White guinea pigs, when interbred with one another, always produce only white. However, if a white female is bred to a black male, the offspring are all black like the father. In its simplest terms, this experiment shows that the sperm cells of the black male carry within them some specific information, some determining factor, in regard to this color. This information is conveyed to cells of the young developing guinea pigs and determines that as the hair grows from the hair follicles it will have black pigment deposited in it. In like fashion, it can be shown that the determiners for the trait may be transmitted equally well through the egg.

Analysis of inheritance depends to a very great degree on experiments which permit us to prove just what is and what is not transmitted from one generation to the next. Beginning with the work of Gregor Mendel [1] more than a hundred years ago, the following essential truths about inheritance have been discovered, mostly by the use of breeding experiments.

What the fertilized egg inherits with respect to a trait like coat color in guinea pigs is a pair of nuclear determinants dealing with that trait. One of this pair is brought in from the father via the sperm (which is all nucleus) and the other from the mother in the nucleus of the egg. The fertilized egg has both of these determinants in its nucleus. They are handed down as the fertilized egg divides, and all the cells which are directly descended from it get duplications of these determinants. In this manner, the hair-forming cells come to have the same determinants which were present at fertilization.

The determinants are called the genes, or the gene pairs. The genes have a number of striking and unexpected features. First, they are discrete units which do not blend but remain permanently separate units which can be recognized individually. They are ordinarily unchanged from generation to generation. They are located on the chromosomes. The latter when stretched out, that is, uncoiled, are long slender threads, each one holding a lineup of genes, numbering in the hundreds, from one end to the other.

It has always been very tempting to picture the genes as if they were beads lined up on a string, necklace fashion. This is one of the initial and rather crude analogies which was made when these facts were first coming to light. Like most attempts at analogy, it is a very great oversimplification, especially with regard to the action of the genes in producing their particular effects.

As will be discussed later, the analogy to a coded system like a tape recording is better than to a string of beads. Nevertheless, the "string of beads" view of the structure of the chromosome, temporarily held, helps to dispel a number of views which we now know to be wholly wrong. One of these was the idea that inheritance blends the contributions of the two parents indistinguishably. The genes are not fluids or droplets capable of such blending; they are particles in the sense that they can be separated from one another and then put back together again. The genes do not come and go, disintegrate and reappear; they have a permanent nature and can change only very rarely. The genes are not something apart from life; they are indeed a part of the living fiber itself. They have the property unique to life, that is, they can make duplicates of themselves.

A simple breeding experiment

For a given character, for example, coat color in guinea pigs, an individual normally has a single pair of major determiners, that is, two separate genes located on two separate chromosomes. Let us represent a gene which results in white hair by the symbol w (read this as "small w"). Now, because of the "two-dose" rule, a white-haired guinea pig must have two w genes in each of its cells. Each of these genes is working in the same direction on hair color, that is, towards the production of white hair. The basic genetic formula of such an animal, representing its underlying genic condition, would be written ww. Such a formula is called the genotype.

This same pair of positions on the same pair of chromosomes can be shown, in a completely black strain of guinea pigs, to be occupied by a pair of genes each of which is slightly different from the w ones. These will be represented by W (read as "large W"). A guinea pig having two doses of W, that is, which has the genotype WW, will appear black. In more detail, this means that the presence of the W determiners in the cells somehow works for the production of black pigment, making the hair of the animal black.

A diagram of the cross between white and black, is given in Fig. 5. This simple cross illustrates a number of important principles of inheritance. In the first place, each parent carries a pair of genes with respect to this character of whiteness or black-

THE HEREDITARY INFORMATION 17

ness of hair. These are in all body cells of each animal and are represented in the figure as being located on a pair of chromosomes; this is superimposed on a silhouette of the animal. When the female produces an egg, however, special movements of the chromosomes occur and only one of this pair makes its way into the young egg cell. The white mother, having only genes of the

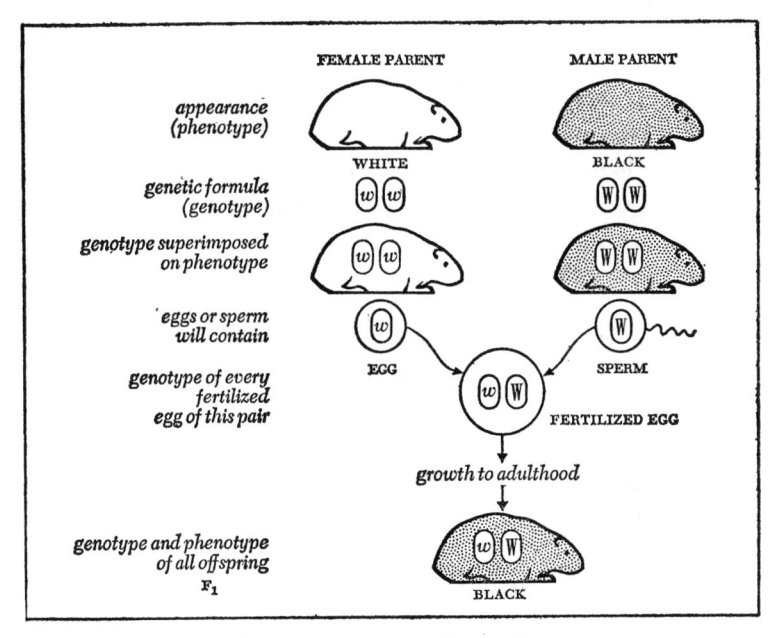

Fig. 5. Inheritance of coat color in the guinea pig

Symbols: W, a gene on a chromosome which will work to produce black pigment, that is, will lead to black hair; w, a gene which will prevent the formation of pigment, that is, will lead to white hair.

w type, can only produce eggs with a single w gene. The process occurring in sperm formation is fundamentally the same. The black father, being WW, can only produce sperm of the W type.

When the fertilized egg is formed, represented in Fig. 5 by

the arrows joining the contributions made by egg and sperm, the individual of the next generation (the F_1 or "first filial generation") gets one of each kind of gene from his parents. His genotype is therefore Ww, but what will his coat color be? In this case it turns out to be black. This is due to a property of the W gene; it has an action which completely dominates, during development, the action of the w gene when the two are present together in the same individual. We say, therefore, that W, the gene for black, is dominant and w, the gene for white, is recessive. Whether a gene is dominant or recessive has to be determined, by experiment or observation, in each case. White coat color in cats, for instance, is due to a dominant gene, whereas most whites in mammals are recessive genes leading to albinism.

To return to the case of the guinea pigs shown in Fig. 5, it is important to note that although the father and his offspring look alike (they are both black) they differ in their genotypes. The father has two doses of the dominant gene, whereas his offspring, having a white mother, all carry the gene for white in the hidden form. A recessive gene shows up and causes a detectable effect only when it is present in double dose. Only a single dose is needed for a dominant gene to express itself. Almost every individual carries genes which he himself does not show. His offspring may not show them either, but the possibility is always present that in some later generation two such recessive genes might get together by having the appropriate egg and sperm meet in a fertilized egg. The character, which otherwise might be thought to be completely lost or diluted by crossing, turns up in its original form, unchanged by even a long sojourn in the hidden form.[2]

This basic principle can be seen if we trace the events which occur when a cross is made between two of the black "carrier" guinea pigs which were produced in the example given in Fig. 5. We now carry the experiment through another generation by mating sister and brother guinea pigs to produce the F₂ (second filial) generation (Fig. 6). Consider first the sister, who now becomes a female parent. Unlike her mother, her genotype will be Ww. As has been stressed earlier, she can put only one of the two chromosomes carrying a coat-color gene into any one egg.

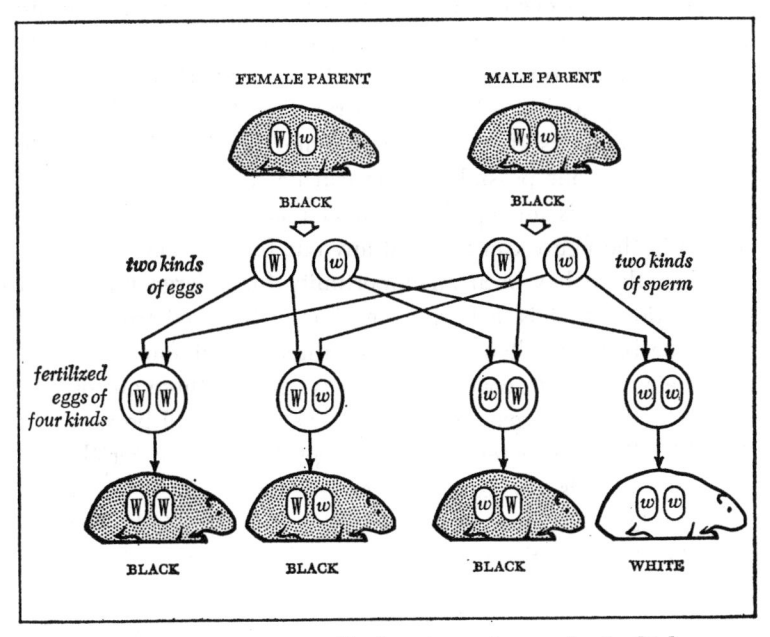

Fig. 6. *Mating of two black guinea pigs, each of which is a carrier of the gene for white*

Symbols: W, black; w, white.

Each time an egg is formed, one of these is put into it and the other discarded. She therefore forms two kinds of eggs, one with W and one with w. As the choice of which one is transmitted and which one discarded is made wholly by chance each time and the chance of each getting in is the same, half the eggs she forms will contain W and the other half w.

In the male, exactly the same principle holds: sperm are produced half of which include W and half of which contain w. A single ejaculation of the male sperm might contain some millions of sperm, but we can show that if we take just one of these cells at random it is equally likely to contain W or w.

These chance events in the formation of eggs and sperm are followed by a second chance event, the union of just one egg and just one sperm to form each fertilized egg. If there are two kinds of eggs and two kinds of sperm, then there are two times two or four ways that these can come together. Referring to Fig. 6, these four possible events can be seen by following the arrows. There is an equal likelihood that any one of the four shown in the figure can result at any one fertilization.

When there has been an opportunity for a large number of fertilizations, that is, a fairly large family is raised from such a pair, the basic result may be seen: three out of four are black like their parents in coat color. This is because three out of four get at least one W gene. One out of every four will be ww, that is, white like the maternal grandparent. The reason for the appearance of this 3:1 ratio is clear when we follow, in Fig. 6, the way in which the two kinds of eggs and two kinds of sperm combine to form the fertilized eggs. The genotypes will occur in a ratio of one WW to two Ww to one ww.[3] Because WW and Ww cannot be distinguished by looking at the animals, only the ratio of three black to one white can be directly observed in the experiment as described here. In practice, further breeding tests with the black animals are necessary to prove how many of them are WW and how many Ww.

This example of the mode of inheritance of a simple recessive gene illustrates what is perhaps the most common mode of inheritance in living things, including man. The recessive nature of many genes helps explain why grandparental characters often reappear after apparently skipping a generation. As mentioned earlier, the genes causing the character have in no way been changed by being hidden by their corresponding dominants for one or even many generations. The double-dose condition, when reformed by the fusion of the appropriate egg and sperm, is accompanied by a full reappearance of the character in undiluted form.

The determination of sex

In man, there are 46 chromosomes; these comprise 23 pairs. This is illustrated in Fig. 7, where the chromosomes, normally scattered throughout the nucleus, have been cut out of a photograph similar to that in Fig. 4 and arranged on the page in such a way as to illustrate the pairs. A number of simple recessive traits are known to have their gene pairs located on one of these chromosome pairs. A recessive gene resulting in albinism, for instance, is located on one of them and can be shown to be inherited in a manner exactly like the one causing white coat color in guinea pigs in the earlier example.

One pair of chromosomes is quite distinctive both in its appearance under the microscope and in one of its major effects. These are the "sex chromosomes," so called because genes on them are instrumental in directing the development of the fertilized egg either towards maleness or femaleness, although they carry additional genes dealing with characters unrelated to sex. The sex chromosome pair in a male individual consists of two unlike chromosomes, called X (the larger) and Y (the smaller) (Fig. 7). In the female, the Y chromosome is absent, but is replaced by a second X chromosome. The positive role in this situation is played by the Y chromosome, which, if present in a fertilized egg, has strong male-determining tendencies. In its absence, development goes towards femaleness.

The mode of sex determination in humans is shown in Fig. 8. When eggs are formed, a female puts into each egg only one kind of chromosome with respect to sex determination, that is,

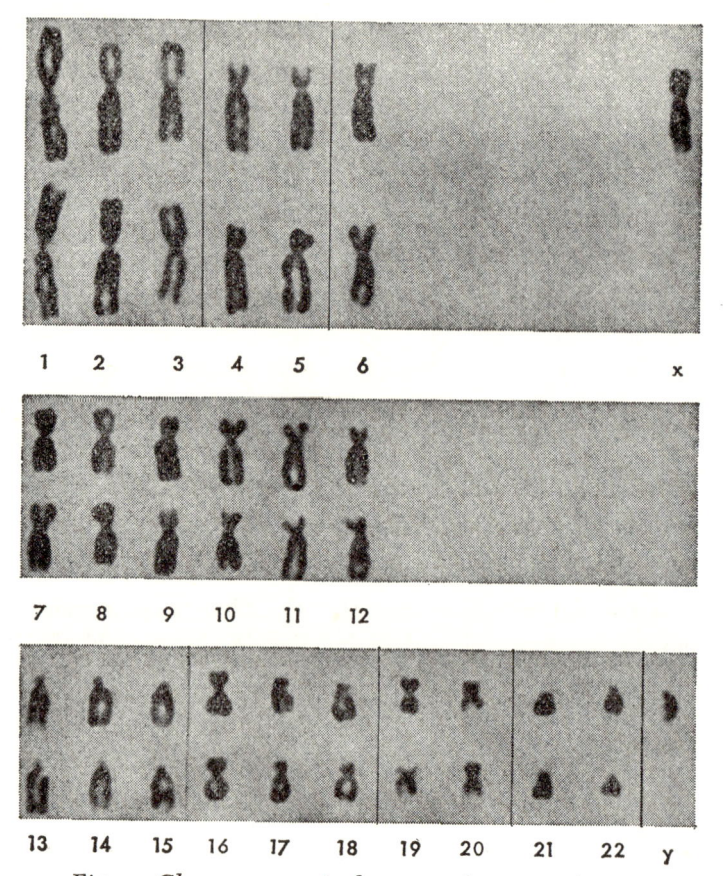

Fig. 7. Chromosomes of a human male arranged so as to show the existence of pairs

In pairs 1–22, the two members of each pair are the same shape and length; they correspond exactly. In pair 23 of the male, the two members are dissimilar, consisting of a single larger X chromosome and a smaller Y chromosome. Figure courtesy of Dr. J. H. Tjio.

an X chromosome. The male, on the other hand, will put an X into one half of the sperm and a Y into the other half. The arrows in the figure denote the results from the chance combination of the two kinds of sperm with the one kind of egg. If a Y sperm happens to reach the egg at a particular fertilization, the result will be a boy, that is, the fertilized egg will be XY, like the father.

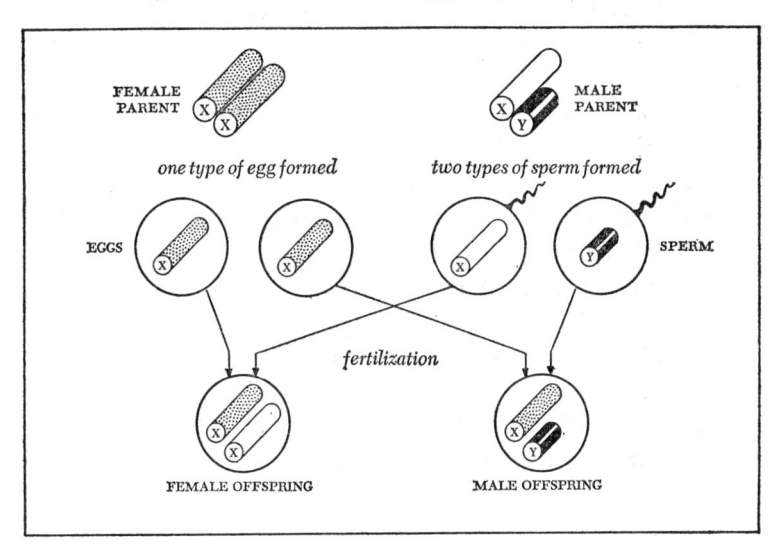

Fig. 8. Sex determination in man

Conversely, the father's X combined with the mother's X will give an XX fertilized egg, which will develop into a girl.[4]

In man, the X chromosome seems to be rather passive in sex determination, as can be inferred from a number of interesting cases of abnormal distributions of chromosomes. Thus, in the formation of the egg, for example, a very rare "error" may occur. Instead of one X, the egg may get two from the female parent, that is, neither one is thrown away, as normally happens. One result is the possible formation of an XXY fertilized egg; this will occur when one of the abnormal XX eggs is fertilized by a normal Y-bearing sperm. Individuals who grow up having the XXY condition have 47 chromosomes rather than the normal 46. They develop into sterile intersexes, although they have mostly male characteristics, apparently due to the strong male-determining influence of the Y chromosome. Persons having one X and no Y (so-called XO individuals) have been recognized by chromosomal examination. They have 45 chromosomes and, like the 47-chromosome persons, are sterile. In this instance, however, the absence of the Y chromosome apparently leads to development in a female direction because such individuals have generally a female appearance despite the fact that they are anatomically somewhat abnormal. A single case of a person with three X chromosomes has been recorded. This person, although sterile, was female in appearance. A person with a Y chromosome but no X should theoretically be occasionally formed but might not be expected to live in the complete absence of X chromosome genes. No such case has been found.

Although sterility, in the technical sense of being unable to have children, is frequently one of the conditions associated with abnormal sex chromosome constitutions, the condition can result from many other things as well. Thus sterility is frequently found in men or women who are wholly normal anatomically and in sex chromosome constitution.

Gene action

In addition to making more of itself, a remarkable enough feat, living material can perform the chemical synthesis of hundreds of special, complex substances. These substances perform many delicate and intricate functions which characterize the living state.

Very recently, the special part played by the hereditary material in the formation of these substances has become clear. Living material includes three general classes of special compounds: fats, carbohydrates, and proteins. The more we study the functions of living material the more prominent a role we must ascribe to the proteins. In a very real sense they make living material what it is. The things that the mature living being does, all the way from the visual sensation by which food is recognized to the final burning within the cell of the food as fuel, involve an extraordinary series of complex chemical reactions involving thousands of proteins as special participants.

Where do all these special proteins come from? There is definitely not room for all of them in the fertilized egg, so they cannot be directly inherited. They are not found outside of living things, so we cannot suppose that the living being finds them and takes them in as it does water or salts. We can only conclude that the living organism makes them itself.

This brings up the problem of how the living thing "knows" how to make a particular protein which it needs for a particular function. For example, in our bodies and in those of most other vertebrates as well, the major system of burning sugar for energy depends on the participation of a specific and very complicated protein, the hormone insulin.

The fertilized egg contains no insulin, yet certain of the cells descended from the fertilized egg, specifically the so-called "islet" cells of the pancreas, can and normally do synthesize this protein. Is the information as to how to put together this hormone somehow acquired during individual life, or is this part of the coded information passed through the fertilized egg from the previous generation?

The disease diabetes mellitus is characterized by a defective insulin-making mechanism. Studies of pedigrees show that the difference between a person with a normal insulin-manufacturing system and one with a defective system depends on a fairly simple genetic difference, probably a single gene. This gene must provide some sort of model or pattern for a key part in the synthesis of insulin. When this model is damaged or somehow incomplete, the formation of the substance by the cells is correspondingly inadequate or incomplete.

There is very good reason to think that most genes operate by providing the information which the machinery of the cell must have to carry out normally a myriad of daily chemical functions whereby the body both grows and maintains itself. The simpler and more obvious characters which reveal their hereditary nature to our simple inspection, such as hair color and texture, eye color, and skin color, also have a chemical base. In the final analysis, the genes are operating through biochemical pathways.

This is the reason that so much of modern genetics, especially that which deals with the effects of genes in development, requires the use of chemical methods. Just as our whole functioning as an integrated body structure requires continual biochemical action, this action would be unorganized and seriously defective or absent were it not for the direction given to it by the hereditary material.

Hereditary material as coded information

The hereditary material is packaged into a definite number of chromosomal units and consists of many thousands of genes. It provides a coded informational system both for our development from the embryo to the adult and our continued functioning as adults. It is questionable whether any cell could synthesize any of its special proteins without the prior existence of the nucleus inside it as a directing element.

If another analogy may be permitted, what the hereditary material resembles, as far as our modern machine technology is concerned, is a sort of tape recording. All of the complex interactions of sound which can be produced by a symphony orchestra can be coded and transferred to a linear strip of plastic material. Once the information is on the tape, it can be run through a machine which, given this information, can reproduce the symphony with accuracy. Lacking the tape, the playback machine yields only random noise or static.

In this crude analogy, the tape itself is comparable to the hereditary material and the electronic playback device to the environment of the growing living being. Obviously, playback machines are of various quality. With the finest high-fidelity machines the tape information is expressed with the greatest accuracy, however, if there is a defect in the tape, no amount of electronic excellence can compensate for it, although the symphony as a whole may continue. Just as the best over-all performance derives from an excellent tape and an excellent machine to play it on, so the best results in the living realm result from a sound hereditary basis operating in an environment where the important conditions (food, for example) are optimal.

DNA

What sort of chemical substance is it which is found in the nucleus and comprises the physical basis of heredity? The simplest way to answer this question would be to gather a whole lot of cell nuclei, free from the rest of the cell parts, yolk, fat, special proteins, and other extraneous materials, and analyze them chemically. This is a difficult job, but in recent years great strides have been made in precisely such analytical methods.

Early chemical studies of this sort were made on sperm. This was an obvious place to try, because, as we have stressed before, the sperm is virtually all nucleus, if one is willing to overlook the tail parts. More recently, methods have been developed for getting nuclei of various other types of cells (e.g., thymus gland, liver, and blood) in virtually pure preparation so that they can be analyzed. Two things are found: proteins and large amounts of a particularly interesting substance which has been called deoxyribose nucleic acid (DNA, for short). Either protein or DNA, or possibly some combination of the two, must carry the coded information. Efforts have been made in recent years to solve this problem and the evidence is now overwhelming that the specificity lies with the nucleic acid rather than the protein. Obviously, the best way to obtain definitive proof is to eliminate one substance completely and see if the other alone can carry the great specificity characteristic of genes. Only quite recently, highly purified DNA, separated from all but minute traces of associated protein, has been shown to be capable of carrying specific hereditary messages. Although these experiments were carried out on microbial organisms, there is good reason to believe that the conclusions reached apply to all living cells.[5]

To repeat, DNA is the physical basis of the genetic information. This sensational discovery, one which ranks equally alongside the atomic theory and the proof that life comes from life, stands as one of the greatest scientific achievements of our time. It is little wonder that life scientists of many kinds are converging on a detailed study of DNA from the structural, physical, and biochemical points of view. DNA is a giant molecule. Basically, it is a very long and very slender thread; how these threads are arranged on the larger structure of the chromosome is not known at all.

The known facts around DNA seem to place very extraordinary requirements on it as a chemical substance. First, it must be able to store, in some sort of arrangement, the information from which proteins can be made. It must be able, on call, as it were, to direct the formation of these proteins by somehow transferring its special "knowledge" to the machinery in the cell beyond the nucleus. It must be able, periodically, to duplicate itself exactly, down to the uttermost detail of its structure, otherwise it would not have the observed property of constancy.

An elegant theory of the molecular structure of DNA has recently been proposed. It is appealing because it provides a picture which is consistent with almost all of the facts that we have about the hereditary material. In short, it is that a molecule of DNA is formed of two very long threadlike chains which are coiled or wound around one another and are bridged across the middle by other chemical substances called bases. There are four kinds of bases. The order in which they are arranged in the molecule can be almost endlessly varied; they form a basic alphabet from which an almost inconceivable number of combinations can be formed. When chromosome reproduction occurs, the two threads are thought to unwind and simultaneously build alongside themselves daughter threads of precisely identical nature.[6]

This brings us to the present frontier in this subject. These ideas of structure are testable (the measure of worth as far as theories are concerned) but the final answers are not yet available. They are coming, and coming soon. Along with them will come an understanding of just how the information gets to the cell machinery. DNA has already been synthesized from its basic building blocks in the laboratory test tube,[7] and there is a wide feeling of confidence that the knowledge now exists to create new kinds of functional DNA from the basic raw materials of which it is made. If and when this step is achieved, we may fairly say that the central ingredient of life will have been synthesized.

Summary

The hereditary determinants are chromosomal units called genes. Genes do not blend with one another; they behave in inheritance as particles capable of being separated and then recombined without losing their identity, a process analogous to the shuffling and dealing of cards. These laws have been largely worked out by breeding experiments. Characters which are strongly affected by single genes are followed through several generations. Genes determining a single character ordinarily occur in pairs and each member is a part of the actual substance of a chromosome. If the two alternative genes present in a cell are different from one another, the action of one (the dominant) may cover up completely the action of the other (the recessive). This provides a biological façade behind which variability can be hidden. The egg (or sperm) receives only one of the two alternates of each gene. Both this event and the process that determines which egg will fuse with which sperm are governed strictly by the laws of chance.

The hereditary material consists of deoxyribose nucleic acid (DNA) which exists in giant molecules of great specificity. DNA operates by providing detailed coded information, akin to a tape recording or blueprint, whereby the living cell "knows" how to synthesize specific proteins. Such proteins form the functional basis for those characters which have a strong basis in heredity.

Chapter 3

STABILITY OF THE HEREDITARY MATERIAL

THE genetic substance is very stable. As growth of the individual proceeds, a certain lineup of genes may be duplicated and passed, by the mechanisms accompanying cell division, to millions of descendant cells without any change in molecular structure. Often, it can be proved that this stability extends from generation to generation.

Chromosomal reproduction during the division of the cell is the major biological adaptation to the maintenance of the status quo in heredity. It represents a self-copying process which operates with extraordinary regularity to maintain continuity with the past. The connection extends not only to immediate precursor cells but also back through the fertilized eggs of uncounted past generations. Discussions of hereditary change often overlook the pervading power that the hereditary material has for the conservation of its own basic sameness.

Gene mutation

Changes in the hereditary material, however, do occur. The startling nature of these changes and their importance has elicited extraordinary interest in them. The process whereby changes in the genes occur, gene mutation, has quite rightly occupied the center of the stage in genetic study, yet the frequency with which such changes occur is extremely low. The genetic material presents a puzzling paradox: it has extraordinary constancy, yet shows changes.

Detailed studies of mutations have shown that the process whereby they arise has the following attributes. In the first place, the basis of the change is some altered arrangement within the molecular structure of the hereditary material itself, DNA. Each molecule of DNA is extraordinarily large, with many positions where the single chemical alteration we are talking about may occur. The change occurs at a single instant in time, like a small explosion. It is thus a sudden, revolutionary event which is confined to one minute point on the molecule. Only this gene is permanently changed thenceforth. The unmutated member of the pair of genes as well as all the other thousands of genes in the rest of the cell remain unaffected by the change.

Naturally occurring or spontaneous mutations are not only exceedingly rare events, governed by the laws of chance, but, in very many instances, the effects of the newly mutated gene are recessive to the normal condition. These attributes make the recognition of new recessive mutations a difficult problem. For example, let us say that you are the unknown carrier of a recessive gene which arose by mutation several generations ago, perhaps in a reproductive cell transmitted by one of your great-grandparents. This mutant gene could have been passed through a grandparent to one of your parents and thence to you, wholly by chance, without being detected yet. If the gene is a rare one, occurring only occasionally in different hereditary lines, it might be transmitted through quite a few generations more before a chance marriage between two carriers occurred. Under these circumstances, of course, the chance is one out of four that a child showing the effect of the gene in double dose would be born (see Fig. 6).

On the other hand, if the newly mutated gene is dominant

to the nonmutated condition, detection is easy and can be made within a generation of the time of origin of the mutation. The trouble with relying on dominant genes for study is their rarity. An example of such a dominant mutation in man is the gene responsible for the condition known as chondrodystrophic dwarf-

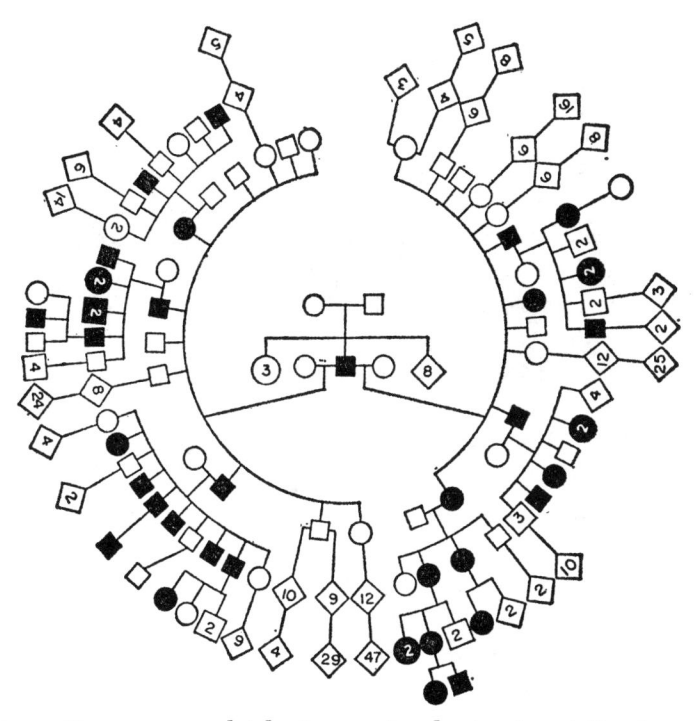

Fig. 9. Occurrence and inheritance of a dominant mutation in man

Circles represent females; squares, males. Individuals affected with the condition chondrodystrophic dwarfism are shown in solid black. The mutation originally occurred in a germ cell giving rise to the man (black square) in the center of the diagram. All other affected individuals in the diagram have inherited this gene from him. (From C. Stern, *Principles of Human Genetics*, San Francisco, W. H. Freeman and Company, Publishers, 1960, 2d ed., p. 448.)

ism. This gene, even when present in single dose, affects the development of the skeleton in such a way that the cartilage areas in the growing bones are abnormal, resulting in a stunting and distortion of the stature of the individual.[1]

Fig. 9 represents a pedigree of a family showing the initial point of mutation and subsequent transmission of the gene for chondrodystrophic dwarfism. In this diagram, males are represented by squares and females by circles. If an individual shows the trait, the symbol is blacked in. Marriages are represented by a line joining the sides of two symbols and the children are shown by a bracket leading to the line below. In this pedigree, large numbers of descendants and marriage partners are known, all of which lack the trait. Notation of this fact has been simplified in the diagram by using a diamond symbol, inside of which the number of normal individuals known is given, without separating sexes or showing marriages.

Beginning at the middle of Fig. 9, then, we see represented a marriage of two normal individuals which resulted in 12 children, of which all were normal but one, a dwarfed boy. This dwarfed individual married twice; his descendants by his first wife are shown to the left and by his second to the right. Of his 22 children, seven were dwarfed, including individuals of both sexes. Inspection of the pedigree shows that no dwarfed individual was subsequently born in this lineage who did not have at least one dwarfed parent, with the exception of the original individual. Study of this and other pedigrees for this trait makes it obvious that the original individual was showing the effects of a new mutation which probably occurred in one sperm or one egg of his parents, either before or at the time of the fertilization which gave rise to him. This was the original mutational event. All the other dwarfs indicated in Fig. 9 inherited replications of this original mutant gene by a scheme which follows the expectations of simple dominant inheritance.

The new occurrence of dominant genes, such as that discussed above, makes it possible to estimate the frequency with which this particular changed gene arises. Rates of mutation are generally given as the number of new mutations that would be expected in a certain number of eggs or sperm. Different genes show different rates of mutation, although variation in these is not so very great. Thus, chondrodystrophy turns out to be among the highest known in man, with about four mutants per 100,000 eggs or sperm. A number of other abnormal genes originate by mutation at lower rates. The gene causing the hereditary bleeding disease hemophilia, for example, shows about two mutants per 100,000 eggs or sperm, whereas the dominant type of muscular dystrophy shows a rate of less than one per 100,000. Huntington's chorea, a mental disorder which develops in later life, appears to show a mutation rate of only one per million.

Special methods of analysis indicate that the rate of mutation to recessive genes is quite similar to that given above for dominant mutations. As has been emphasized, this consideration is important because many recessive genes which arose scores or even hundreds of generations previously may exist in the hereditary material of present-day individuals without showing up. All of us carry mutant genes, mostly in the recessive condition. These are part of our natural hereditary endowment. All of us who have children pass at least some of these genes on to the next generation. More than this, however, somewhere around 30 percent of us contain one newly mutated gene. As will be discussed below, most mutations are somewhat harmful. We are therefore indeed fortunate that detrimental dominant genes are not more frequent in man; the nonmutated members of the gene pairs ordinarily afford us protection of an extremely important sort, by covering up our load of bad recessive genes.

Visible chromosome changes

The type of hereditary change which is exemplified by chondrodystrophic dwarfism involves a change in the molecular structure of the chromosome. Ordinarily, such a change does not affect the ability of the chromosome or the cell nucleus to reproduce itself. Furthermore, microscopic examination of the chromosome shows no detectable difference from the normal chromosome, that is, the one which is unmutated. Obviously, the change is too small to be seen with even the best of our present-day microscopes.

A category of chromosome change is known, however, which does cause visible changes in chromosome structure. The most striking change of this sort occurs when a chromosome becomes broken straight across so that it comes apart into two pieces. Following one or more such breaks, a number of possibilities are open. First, the broken ends may heal back so that no broken chromosomes are found in descendant cells. Second, the broken parts may float away from the main part of the chromosome, forming loose fragments. These fragments, and the genes they contain, are usually lost because they become disconnected from that portion of the chromosome which is necessary for normal chromosome movements during cell division. Loss of even a small fragment of the hereditary material will result in death of a cell.

Figure 10 is a photograph of a human cell which has just divided; the two large dark masses are the daughter groups of chromosomes which have recently moved apart. The stage of division is quite similar to Fig. 3g. Just before division, however, the cell in Fig. 10 was irradiated with a small dose of x rays. Four fragments, due to the breakage of chromosomes, can be seen. Furthermore, a fine chromosome line or "bridge" can be seen connecting the two daughter groups of chromosomes. This is also the result of breakage, followed by refusion of the broken ends in an abnormal way so that the two halves of the chromosome are joined together instead of being separate. When the

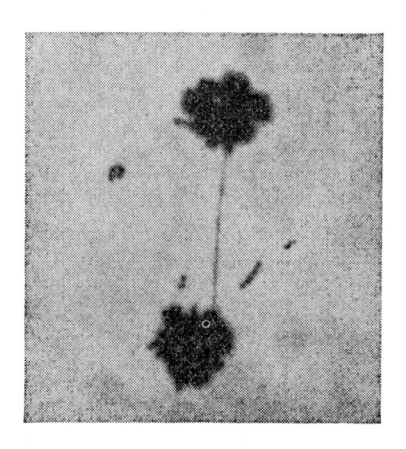

Fig. 10. Radiation damage to a human cell

Photograph of a stained cell in division; the two dark masses are daughter chromosome groups. Just prior to division, the cell was irradiated with 25 r units of x rays. Four fragments of broken chromosome, in addition to a chromosome bridge, have been produced by the treatment. Photograph courtesy of Dr. Norman H. Giles.

two halves of the chromosome try to go their separate ways, they find that they are connected to one another and cannot move apart normally. As a result, they string out a bridge between them. The bridge ultimately breaks and the distribution of the chromosome material is not exact. Accordingly, we would expect both of the cells resulting from the division shown in Fig. 10 to die since they lack normal genes both because of the fragments and the bridge.

When two breaks occur more or less simultaneously in one chromosome, there may be several possible outcomes. Let us diagram these events by first representing the longitudinal arrangement of the genes on a particular chromosome by a series of men's names, thus:

<u>Arthur. .Byron. .Charles. .David. .   etc.</u>

Let us say that the two chromosome breaks, giving four broken chromosome ends marked by asterisks, occur at either end of the name Byron, so that this piece becomes loose, thus:

<u>*.Byron.*</u>
<u>Arthur.*</u>   <u>*.Charles. .David. .   etc.</u>

As indicated above, <u>*.Byron.*</u> may fuse back into the same place that it broke out of, and in the same order. On the other hand, *.Bryon.* may be lost completely and the broken end of <u>Arthur.*</u> may fuse to the beginning of <u>*.Charles. . .</u> The result would be a loss of Byron and probable cell death. On the other hand, it has sometimes been observed that such a fragment as *.Byron.* fuses back in the reversed order, so as to give a chromosome with part of its genes in a new order, thus:

<u>Arthur. ·uoɹʎq· .Charles. .David. .   etc.</u>

Such events are called chromosome inversions and are frequent following multiple breakage.

Another series of events may follow separate breaks occurring in two different chromosomes. This may be represented as follows; each of the two different chromosomes is represented by a different series of names, with the breaks indicated by asterisks as before:

<u>Arthur.*</u>
        <u>*.Byron. .Charles. .David. .   etc.</u>

and

<u>Alice.*</u>
        <u>*.Barbara. .Cora. .Diana. .   etc.</u>

Following movements of the chromosomes and the fragments within the cell, refusion of the parts may take place in the following way:

Alice. .Byron. .Charles. .David. .   etc.

and

Arthur. .Barbara. .Cora. .Diana. .   etc.

Such an event is known as a translocation. Essentially what has happened is that Alice and Arthur have traded places. In the case of both translocations and inversions, the resulting cell often lives perfectly well, temporarily, at least, because nothing is added or lost. The material within the chromosome has been merely rearranged.

A final category of chromosome change, or mutation in the broad sense, may be mentioned. This involves the duplication or loss of one complete member of a chromosome pair without any molecular changes or breakages in the chromosomes. Examples of this kind of chromosome change have previously been considered in the section on sex determination. If an original cell has 46 chromosomes, each daughter should also receive 46, a perfect duplicate set. When the rare accident occurs, however, the cell division involved may result in one cell with 45 and the other with 47. This result would come about if normal separation in one chromosome fails and the unseparated daughters are both included in only one of the two resulting cells, giving a cell with 47. The other cell and, of course, its descendants lack this chromosome entirely and will have only 45 chromosomes.

Complete loss of one chromosome by a cell commonly causes the death of that cell. On the other hand, the presence of an extra chromosome (now actually present in triplicate in the cell instead of the normal duplicate) does not always cause death, but, if the cell lives, the condition is often associated with an abnormal condition of some sort. The effects usually resemble those of a gene mutation, although in this case it is due not to a molecular change but rather to a disturbance of the normal balance of genes in the nucleus.

Only very recently it has been demonstrated that individuals unfortunate enough to have been born with the condition designated as mongolian idiocy possess, in each body cell, a total of 47 chromosomes rather than the normal 46. Studies of samples of the chromosomes of such persons show that one of the smallest chromosomes of the human group is present three times rather than the normal twice.

In their effects, importance, and basic nature, chromosomal mutations involving the above rather conspicuous kinds of changes do not differ much from mutations which involve small chemical alterations in the chromosomes. As will be discussed below, they appear to be caused by quite similar environmental agents, like x rays and certain chemicals.

The harmful nature of most mutations

Mutations tend to be harmful rather than helpful. As has been mentioned previously, their origin is only by the dictates of chance; they never arise as a direct response to a particular need that the living being might have for a changed structure or mechanism. The possibility that a chance change will interfere with the operation of some body function is far greater than the possibility that it will serve to improve some function. Although absolute criteria as to what is beneficial and what is harmful are difficult to set up, the ratio of harmful to helpful mutations is on the order of a thousand to one.

Perhaps the most frequent kind of mutation is a change in a chromosome or gene which has such severe effects that it throws some essential part of the delicately balanced machinery completely out of order. If this happens, the cells containing this "bad" gene either die outright or are so sickly that they cannot multiply as fast as cells which do not have the gene causing this drastic effect. In either case, the cells, or to put it more directly, the individuals carrying the cells, with the bad gene die out or are eliminated from further reproduction. Such genes are called lethals, that is, killers. Lethals may be either dominant, requiring only one gene for the killing effect, or recessive, requiring two doses for this result.

Lethal genes are frequent in animals and plants as well as in man. Many perfectly normal-appearing individuals are carriers of recessive lethal genes. Almost any of the essential functional systems of the body can be the target of a lethal mutation. Some lethals interfere so completely with basic life processes that the new individual may die shortly after fertilization. In other cases, the killing effect may come about through the blood system, kidneys, or brain. Individuals affected by such lethals may die during fetal life and be aborted. In some cases, however, the affected individuals may survive until birth, only to die during childhood.

Lethal genes are difficult to separate from the so-called sublethal genes; these latter permit some survival yet interfere almost completely with reproduction, because the individual carrying them is a chronic invalid. The gene causing one of the types of muscular dystrophy, for example, frequently permits survival until approximately age 20. Such individuals, however, do not transmit these genes to the next generation because no case of an affected person having children has been recorded, although this possibility cannot be excluded.

From the biological point of view, almost none of the categories which we try to erect to classify the effects of harmful mutations is discrete. There is an intergradation from severe lethals which kill in the fertilized egg to genes which cripple permanently but do not kill to those whose effects can be relatively easily countered by medication. Thus, the gene resulting in diabetes can be rendered almost innocuous through the use of insulin.

Many genes carried by perfectly normal persons have extremely small effects, so small, in fact, that often there is no easy means of recognizing them individually. The geneticist quite naturally selects for study those mutations which have large effects. It is perhaps for this reason that the nongeneticist, looking at a textbook of genetics, may get the erroneous impression that the genetics of man concerns itself only with the inheritance of large abnormalities. Mutations with slight effects can alter almost any structure of the body. It may cause a slight change in size, shape, color, or texture of some superficial external feature. Very slight alterations may likewise be made in some proportion of the bones of the skeleton (thus an effect on height, for instance) or in internal organs such as glands, teeth, or muscle arrangements. Many of the minor differences which characterize us as individuals have a basis in the genes; these need not be the causative agents of hereditary disease to claim our attention. Many of these changes may be more or less neutral from the point of view of the general health of the individual, some may render him slightly stronger or weaker than the average.

To function normally, the body cells must be able to manufacture, through chemical synthesis, thousands of special chemical substances. These interact in a complex way to produce the result that we recognize as normality. A gene which has been impaired or changed slightly may no longer carry the proper coded message with respect to the manufacture of a particular chemical substance. This lack, or impairment, then, may be expressed in some chemical malfunction.

Most interesting and important in this regard are genes which in their action affect the metabolism of the body. Metabolism refers to the enormously complex collection of biochemical events which is concerned with the conversion of food to energy and to body components. Biologists who study metabolism, that is, the functioning of living material as a system for gathering, utilizing, and holding energy, have documented the chemical reactions which go on in great detail. A given gene may have an action which specifically impairs some metabolic function; such a gene results in an "inborn error of metabolism." The example of diabetes mellitus, mentioned earlier, is a very good one, but, again, to have an important influence, a gene does not need to be as dramatic or severe in its effects as this.

Genes are known to dictate the formation of certain proteins, and it is not surprising to find that the very complex family of proteins in the blood have attracted a lot of attention. Just as two persons, even brothers or sisters, are likely to differ in eye and hair color, so also are they likely to differ to some degree in the type of special chemicals that they would carry in their blood. The presence or the absence of such substances has been shown to be inherited in a relatively simple manner. This fact, coupled with the ease and accuracy with which a chemical test for the presence of a particular chemical can be made, has led to the very widespread use of such hereditary characters as markers in human inheritance.

Knowledge that chemical differences exist dates back to 1901, when the so-called "A-B-O" blood groups were discovered. Genes that stand behind the particular chemical substances in the cells dictate the nature of an individual's blood; they specify what his blood type will be. The direct medical benefits of this discovery were of course connected with avoiding accidents during blood transfusion, that is, being sure that two bloods will not cross-react. But, quite beyond this, blood-group genes serve as superb simple examples of hereditary factors in man. Although the I gene locus, the various alternatives of which are responsible for specifying mucopolysaccharides of the A-B-O group, is the classical one, at least eight other blood-group systems are now known. There are also genes that specify an abnormal type of hemoglobin, the red oxygen-carrying protein of the blood cell. Among the blood-group genes are the L genes, which specify substances M and N and the Rh genes which determine the presence (so-called Rh-positive) or absence (Rh-negative) of still other chemicals. Although in these latter genes some cases result in an incompatibility of the blood of a mother and the genetically different fetus that she may carry, most of these protein differences (excluding the abnormal hemoglobins) may be looked upon as quite minor matters leading to no direct ill effects but serving as interesting examples of minor biochemical differences between individuals.

Although many mutations seem to us to be extremely drastic in their effects, none destroys or changes the basic humanness of the individual suffering its effects. Hereditary idiocy, anemia, blindness, or dwarfism may result from only the most minor change at one point on the genetic information itself. The long historical process whereby the delicately balanced hereditary material capable of developing into a human being arose cannot be reversed by a single event of chance.

Causes of mutations

What causes the molecular change in DNA that we call the gene mutation? A certain very low rate of mutational change occurs spontaneously, and appears to be a natural process, a part of our biological legacy. Evidence is very strong that mutations arise because some agent external to the living cell interferes with the self-copying process that we have discussed previously. Instead of an exact duplicate, an incomplete or slightly changed copy is made and thereafter perpetuated.

Production of mutations experimentally in plants and animals was first demonstrated using x-radiation.[2] The methods which may be used to show this are fairly simple. Young adult animals or plants may be dosed with x rays and then bred with non-irradiated mates. It is usually not difficult to arrange the cross so that the appearance of new hereditary changes caused by the radiation treatment can be recorded in a later generation. All types of radiation, from those with low penetration like ultraviolet rays to atomic radiations such as gamma rays and alpha rays, can be shown to increase the "normal" mutation rate sharply.

Radiation causes a mutation by first causing a molecular change. One of the bits of energy from the radiation source causes an ionization to occur inside the living cell. This change sets up an unstable internal condition which may result in damage to, or rearrangement of, a particular spot on the lineup of genes on a chromosome. Chromosome breaks probably arise in the same way (Fig. 10).

Mutations caused by radiation do not differ in kind from the "spontaneous" ones. The popular conception holds that radiation may result in hitherto unknown and fearful monstrous conditions. This is not so. What would be induced in man would be merely more of the familiar kinds of defects, muscular dystrophy, anemia, idiocy, and blindness.

Like "spontaneous" mutations, experimentally induced ones occur at random. This fact again serves to emphasize the role of chance in hereditary change. This is not surprising because radiations are essentially invisible bullets of energy, so that the radiation of the cell is analogous to shooting at it with a shotgun shell. Each pellet of shot may be said to represent one ray; although, to be more accurate, only certain types of radiations are actually made up of particles. In other equally mutagenic types of radiation, the energy is in electromagnetic form.

When radiation is sprayed at a cell, much of the energy passes right on through it, as in the case of many of the rays used to take an x-ray photograph. These rays may do no harm to the living material at all. The more the radiation, however, the greater the chance that one or more rays will cause a damaging ionization near enough to the hereditary material to affect it and cause a change.

As we have pointed out, mutations have a very large chance of being harmful. Questions which come up at this point are crucial ones for the atomic age. How much radiation is needed to cause a mutation? Is there a dose of radiation which is "safe" in the sense that no mutations at all will be produced?

All the meaningful experimental work on this point indicates that the number of mutations produced is proportional to the dose. The greater the radiation, the more mutations will be produced. The possibility exists, furthermore, that a mutation may be caused by a single ionization, an event which could be caused by one ray.

To return to the shotgun analogy: let us visualize a large marksman's target with concentric rings around a small center bull's-eye. Let us say that a pellet through the bull's-eye represents the induction of a mutation and that pellets passing through the target at other points are harmless. Let us shoot with a shotgun at this target from a fairly great distance, say about 40 yards. What is our chance of hitting the bull's-eye, remembering that we cannot aim the shot accurately; the principle of the shotgun is to spray the pellets generally in the direction of the object. Obviously, success depends on the number of pellets per shell, the accuracy of our aim, and the number of times we shoot.

The effects of low-level radiation can be imagined in this model by considering that we shoot at the target only once a week using a shotgun shell which is blank except for a single pellet of shot. The probability of this unaimed shot striking the bull's-eye is very low, yet the possibility that a single shot could indeed do it must be realized.

If our goal, therefore, is to avoid the mutagenic effects of ionizing radiation, we may conclude that the less radiation we receive the better. The cells which must be protected from the point of view of future generations are specifically eggs and sperm, as well as the cells which are their immediate precursors and are found in the testis and ovary, respectively. The fertilized egg and early embryonic stages are also important because a mutation caused in one cell at an early stage will be transmitted to many descendant cells, some of which might become included into testis or ovary of the adult derived from that fertilized egg.

If the reproductive age of an individual is past, and no possibility of further reproduction exists, then mutations which might occur would die with the individual and not be passed on to future generations. In the light of our present knowledge, the germ cells in the reproductive organs of young people should be afforded as much protection as possible from radiations of all kinds, especially between the time of fertilization and age 30. This latter is taken as the age after which reproduction, on the average, declines.

Natural radiation from rocks, soil, and elsewhere, including cosmic radiation, is not enough to be responsible for all the mutations that may be observed in animals and plants. Radiation, therefore, is by no means the only cause of mutation. In recent years, a large variety of chemical substances, most particularly mustard gas and related substances, have been shown to give rise to mutations under experimental conditions. To cause the effect, the chemicals must get into the cells in the right amount and without damaging them too severely.

The problem of genetic health

The problem of genetic health has two aspects. First, there is the genetic hazard, which concerns damage to the permanent store of human genetic material, over many generations. When reproductive cells are damaged by mutation, the cost, which is represented by the birth of a defective individual, is largely deferred and will not be felt until some later generation. This is, of course, because almost all new changes in heredity are recessive. The human species, through every individual human being, already carries quite a load of detrimental mutations, some of which are always coming out in any one generation. Additions to this load will increase the cost that must be paid by some future generation. In simple human terms, the cost that this load exacts is in the years of mental anguish and physical labor of parents who must care for an individual who is defective from birth.

The second aspect of genetic health concerns itself with medical problems. In this instance, we are concerned primarily with damage to the hereditary mechanisms within the body cells of present-day living individuals, that is, you and me. If these mechanisms or the hereditary materials are seriously damaged, this can give rise to disease. Such diseases can be as crippling and as serious as those caused by infectious agents, bacteria, viruses, or any such agent which invades the body from the outside.

The most startling and significant fact in this field is that the same radiations and chemicals which cause mutation effects when applied to egg and sperm can cause cancer when applied to the nonreproductive cells of the body. Cancer is not one disease but many. Numerous complex and puzzling aberrations of normal maintenance and growth of the body find themselves grouped together under this term.

In the origin of cancer, some change occurs in a cell, somewhere in the body, which is, like a mutation, irreparable. The changed condition is passed along from mother to daughter cell with the same accuracy as an hereditary change. A line of cells, grown in a test tube, will retain their specific cancerous character for years. For all we know, they may remain this way indefinitely. These correlations seem to be more than coincidence; they have led to the theory, not yet proved, that cancer is basically a disease or disability of some part of the hereditary material of the affected body cells. Its cause may be a mutation in the precursors of the changed body cells, manifesting itself in disorganized growth processes and disturbed metabolic functions.

The cancer-inducing effects of radiations are almost never immediately observed. The basic change from normal to cancerous cell may have taken place many years before the tumor which grows from this changed cell appears. This long lag, or latent period, makes the study of the rate of cancer caused by a certain irritant or radiation a very difficult and time-consuming matter. It is easy, also, to underestimate a factor like radiation, low doses of which have not any apparent immediate effect and which we cannot see, feel, smell, or sense directly in any way. This is true of even very large doses.

Whether we are justified in referring to cancer as a genetic disease or not, this approach is now widely accepted as the most promising modern frontier of cancer research. The facts make it inescapable that the hereditary material is closely involved, whether it turns out that the change from normal to cancerous cell is a matter of simple mutation or whether some other more complex change, or series of changes, are involved.

For a hundred years we have known that microorganisms are a prominent cause of disease. Acceptance by the citizens of the world of public health measures such as sanitation came slowly. Even so brilliant a scientist and eloquent a spokesman as Pasteur met with skepticism, ridicule, and disbelief long after his major discoveries of infectious agents of diseases had been confirmed and widened by hundreds of following scientists. The fact that some diseases are nutritional, that is, that disease can arise because something important like a vitamin is missing from the diet, was another recent discovery that met with very hesitant acceptance at first.

That cancerous diseases as well as debilitating and serious mutational events may be caused by simple physical forces such as radiation and certain irritating chemicals is now proved beyond any shadow of a doubt. In making such a statement, we do not say that the disease will always develop or always be severe; just as certain infectious agents may be mild in their effects, so may certain of the genetic diseases. The public mind seems to be obsessed with the idea that "the cause of cancer" is what we seek to know. Once we know, this reasoning runs, that it is caused by "X," then we can simply eliminate X. Cancer is not a single disease. There is no single cause. There are at least a dozen different ways to cause a cancerous growth on the skin of a mouse. We know the causative agents which will do this. We know also that they are operative in human cancer. Conquering many cancers can be begun right now, one step at a time, by avoiding precisely those agents which are known to elicit cancer directly.

One often hears the statement that the increase in radiation through the use of x rays for diagnosis, fallout from atomic explosions, or from wastes of atomic reactors is not sufficient to constitute any genetic or medical hazard. The term "harmless" is frequently used. Now, it is perfectly true that the probability of damage by a low-level source of radiation is much less than that which produces more radiation. Again, let us employ the shotgun analogy. Suppose that you are in the range of a shotgun which is being fired continually, day and night. Your risk is represented by the possibility of a pellet striking you in a vital spot. Obviously, the only situation under which you run no risk of being hit is when the shell being fired is a complete blank, with no shot at all, or when you are completely and permanently out of range of the shot. As soon as you move within range, even though each shell is loaded by only a single pellet and fired from a great distance, the remoteness of your risk does not prevent it from being a real one. This is true even though it is quite possible that you might live out your whole existence in such a situation without ever being struck at all by a pellet. But there is a possibility, that even the very first shot, just by chance, could strike the vital spot.

As pointed out previously, all of us have always been subjected to low-level natural radiation, in fact the human species evolved under it. This does not mean, however, that there has not been any harm from it. Many of the bad recessive genes that we now carry in our hereditary material may have been caused by natural radiation in past generations. In the modern world, however, sources of radiation have been increased and it is important for us to determine the degree to which the threat to genetic health is proportionately greater.

In countries where medical practice is quite advanced, the use of fluoroscopes and x-ray machines for diagnosis and therapy is the most significant new source of radiation that an individual gets. The evidence is overwhelming that large doses of rays from these sources increase the possibility of injury to genetic health. The answer is that we should use x rays only where their use is critical and essential to diagnosis and treatment of an important diseased condition. This puts the responsibility directly on the doctor. He must be aware of the reality of genetic and medical hazards and so be able to weigh the importance of the diagnosis against the possibility of harm caused by the rays. It goes without saying that trivial use of x rays, such as machines which are used for fitting shoes, is highly unsound and should under all circumstances be discontinued.

As indicated, x rays only affect those who voluntarily use them, and the individual person can usually avoid unnecessary amounts. This is not true with regard to the other major source of man-produced radiation which reaches human populations, namely, fallout from atomic explosions. When hydrogen or atomic explosions occur, a large number of radioactive particles are formed. A lot of these particles fall back locally near the site of the explosion. Large amounts of fine radioactive dust particles, however, may be blown up into either the upper atmosphere or stratosphere. From here they drift around the earth generally in the latitude of the explosion and thereafter slowly fall down to earth again, being precipitated in rain in all parts of the earth.

This global fallout from weapons tests constitutes the first general increase in radioactive exposure that the human species has ever encountered, and it is essential to know how much radiation dose an individual gets and what the details are. Many of the radioactive elements produced in the explosion lose their activity in seconds, minutes, or hours after the detonation. Some of them, however, like radiostrontium, decay only very slowly. It takes about 30 years for this element to lose half of its activity. Radiostrontium, sometimes called strontium-90, has other properties that render it dangerous. When precipitated by rain to the surface of the earth again, considerable amounts of it fall on green leaves, especially grass. Strontium is very similar to the element calcium which plays such an important role in living processes. Most living things, including ourselves, accumulate calcium (lime) and build it into cell systems and, of course, bones. Curiously, most living things do not distinguish between strontium and calcium; they therefore take up the strontium-90 with avidity, especially in areas where calcium is normally in short supply.

Some of the strontium-90, then, will be built into the very substance of the grass plant cells. If the plant is corn, wheat, or rice, for example, it may become concentrated in the grain. If the grass is eaten by a cow, the radioactive element can make its way into the cow's bones and into the cow's milk. When drunk, the milk is a source of strontium-90 for human beings; it makes its way into the tissues, especially the bones, along the same path that bone-building calcium takes. Strontium from contaminated grain products acts similarly. Through all this cycle, the strontium continues to emit its stream of radioactive bullets, subjecting its immediate surroundings to continual bombardments of this unfelt, unseen energy.

As most of the strontium-90 is concentrated in the bones, it follows that the damage may be expected to appear there. Large doses of strontium-90 can cause bone cancer and leukemia (a type of blood cancer) in mice. Until we can prove that the very low levels so far due to radiostrontium from atmospheric explosions are indeed harmless, we must make the assumption that all radiation reaching the body cells increases the risk of these diseases.

The risk of cancer from fallout radiation, that is, the medical hazard, at the moment seems greater than the genetic threat to the germ cells. This is because the highest radiation levels due to strontium-90 are received by the bone and blood cells, not by sperm or egg. It is as hard to assess the exact effects on the latter as it is on the former; that some mutations will be directly traceable to fallout radiation, however, is an inescapable conclusion.

This account has dealt primarily with strontium-90 because this element appears to have the most dangerous combination of properties of all the radioactive materials produced by atomic explosions. Megaton hydrogen explosions, however, result in the production of considerable quantities of radiocarbon, carbon-14, which is likewise distributed in a world-wide manner. This element has an extremely long half-life, on the order of 5,700 years, and its long-range threat to genetic health may exceed that of the shorter-lived radioactive elements.

The newness of this general problem of the contamination of

the atmosphere is underscored by the fact that until 1945, when the first atomic explosion was set off, strontium-90 did not exist in the atmosphere or the crust of the earth. In a real sense, it is a wholly man-made element. At the present time there is no human being who does not have strontium-90 in his bones in minute amounts. Children who have grown up since 1945, and whose bones have been built from foods contaminated with strontium-90, have generally larger amounts than persons who grew up before that time.

The use of atomic energy has posed new problems for our time, problems that man has never faced before. Even if we escape the horrifying realities of nuclear war, peaceful use of atomic energy will exact some biological cost, no matter how carefully the material is handled. These costs must be realistically calculated and weighed against the admittedly tremendous potential benefits inherent in the peaceful uses of atomic energy.

Test explosions in the atmosphere have raised the level of radiation applied to each living individual on earth. The responsibility for perpetrating this use of atomic energy, with the military and political pressures which accompany such testing, lies with political leaders, not with the scientists who made the basic discoveries.

Public information on medical and genetic hazards of radiation has been wholly inadequate. This is especially dangerous in the free world where the choice of leaders lies ultimately with an informed electorate. It seems not too much to ask, in this scientific age, that every elector be informed at least sufficiently so that he will see the necessity for political candidates to be informed in depth on these matters.

Nonsense, pseudoscientific claims with hidden selfish interests behind them, commercial advertisers who blur the truth with an eye to profits, manipulation of facts into bizarre unscientific relationships for any political, personal, religious, or social reason

STABILITY OF HEREDITY

—this is the environment in which the great and real scientific truths must compete.

Summary

At very rare intervals, the hereditary material makes an incomplete copy of a small section of its molecular structure. A whole chromosome may be lost or gained or breaks may occur resulting in losses of chromosome pieces or their reunion in new arrangements. All these changes are permanent events and are called mutations. Mutations may affect almost any external or internal structure or biochemical function. The majority of new mutations are recessive to the original condition and their potential effects are covered up. A new mutation has a high probability of being harmful and many kill the cell in which it occurs (lethal mutation). Although their effects are often far-reaching, as in the genes which cause dwarfism, idiocy, or blindness, single mutations involve a change in only an infinitesimal part of the total hereditary material. No such change, therefore, alters the basic condition of being human.

Ionizing radiations of every kind, as well as certain chemicals, increase the rate of mutation. Radiation-induced changes do not differ in kind from those which occur naturally. Their frequency is directly proportional to the dose. Agents which will induce mutations, as detected in reproductive cells and in individuals descended from them, are the same which can cause cancer to arise in body cells. The hazard from these agents is thus of two kinds. First, the genetic hazard arises from mutations occurring in the reproductive cells; defects due to these will appear mostly in some later generation. Second, the medical hazard arises from direct effects on body cells; defects due to cancer induction appear during the lifetime of the individual and affect him only.

Recognition of the necessity of protecting genetic health from agents which cause mutations and cancer has been slow. Popular inertia is comparable to that which was observed soon after the proof that bacteria could cause disease. Holding genetic disease and its attendant human misery to a minimum is directly correlated with holding exposure to damaging radiations and chemicals to a similar minimum.

Chapter 4

COMBINATIONS AND
RECOMBINATIONS OF GENES

Chromosome pairs

CLOSE study of the chromosomes shows that the characteristic number for humans, 46, is actually a double number. This total can always be paired off, by inspection, into 23 groups of two each, as was done in the photograph of a cell of the male individual in Fig. 7. The members of each pair resemble each other in size and shape and this correspondence can be shown to extend down to minute details. Basically, then, the human has 23 kinds of chromosomes, not 46. These are numbered from 1 to 23, and grouped according to size. Pairs of chromosomes match exactly except in the case of the XY pair in the male, the members of which are dissimilar in size and gene content.

Normal persons always have one pair of each kind of chromosome. Where do the two members of each pair come from? The answer is very simple: one member of each pair comes from the father's sperm and the other member from the mother's egg. This is illustrated in Fig. 11, which is a diagrammatic tracing of the photograph of human chromosomes shown earlier in Fig. 4. The pairs are numbered; the chromosomes of paternal origin are on the left in outline, whereas those of maternal origin are shown as solid.

A number of important facts are emphasized by the paired

58   COMBINATIONS OF GENES

condition of the chromosomes. In the first place, it can be seen that a parent never contributes all of his chromosomes to one of his offspring. Specifically, he contributes 23, an exact half-set. This always consists of one member of each of the 23 pairs, not

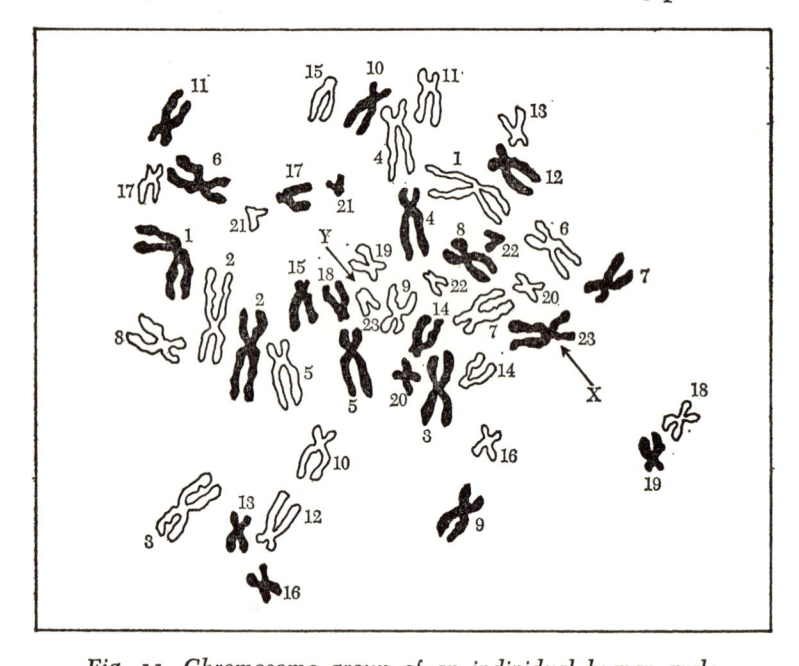

Fig. 11. Chromosome group of an individual human male

Traced from Fig. 4. Chromosomes come equally from each parent. Of his chromosomes, 23 came from his mother (blacked in) and 23 came from his father (open). Thus, chromosomes come in pairs, one member of each pair coming from each parent (see also Fig. 7).

just any 23 chromosomes of the 46. The new individual thus never derives his whole chromosomal constitution from either one of his parents; he represents a new combination of chromosomes derived from the two sources. This means, of course, that in the formation of the egg and sperm there must be a special process whereby the chromosome number that the reproductive cell carries is reduced from 46 to 23, and done in such a way that just one representative of each pair arrives in the final cell.

Let us diagram a cross in which the chromosomes of the male parent may be represented thus:

$$1\text{-}1 \quad 2\text{-}2 \quad 3\text{-}3 \ldots 23\text{-}23; \text{ total, } 46$$

and the female parent:

$$\underline{1\text{-}1} \quad \underline{2\text{-}2} \quad \underline{3\text{-}3} \ldots \underline{23\text{-}23}; \text{ total, } 46$$

The pairs are represented by their numbers and the underscore in this case makes it possible to distinguish the contribution of the female from that of the male. At reproduction, then, we observe the following:

male parent 1-1 2-2 3-3 . . . 23-23 × female parent $\underline{1\text{-}1}$ $\underline{2\text{-}2}$ $\underline{3\text{-}3}$ . . . $\underline{23\text{-}23}$

male sperm   1   2   3 . . . 23 × female egg $\underline{1}$ $\underline{2}$ $\underline{3}$ . . . $\underline{23}$

offspring 1-$\underline{1}$ 2-$\underline{2}$ 3-$\underline{3}$ . . . 23-$\underline{23}$

This diagram illustrates that the offspring has an unchanged total number, the chromosomes are still present in pairs; one member of each pair comes from his father and the other from his mother.

Formation of eggs and sperm

Quite obviously, from the foregoing, sperm and egg cannot be produced by the usual processes of mitosis, but must originate by some rather special process—one which assures that the number is halved at the same time that one member of each chromosome pair is preserved. Detailed microscopical study of the cellular events that go on during the formation of the egg or sperm have shown that these results are accomplished during two rather specialized and complex cell and nuclear divisions. These divisions, called meiosis, or "lessening," are confined strictly to certain cells of the testis or the ovary which ultimately give rise to the sperm or eggs. Under the microscope these divisions su-

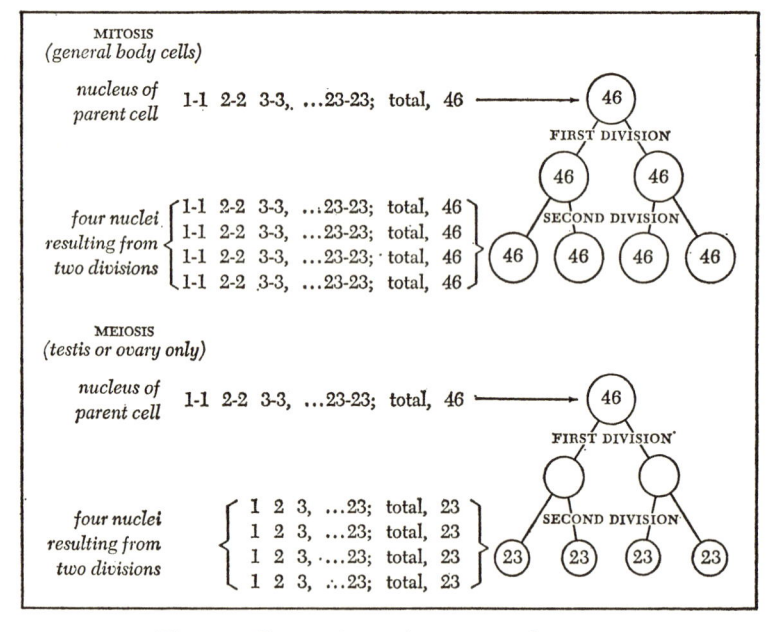

Fig. 12. Comparison of mitosis and meiosis

perficially resemble mitosis but have results which are quite different.

Mitosis, it will be recalled, always maintains exactly in all descendant nuclei the precise conditions that were present in the parent nucleus. Meiosis reduces the number of chromosomes and sorts out the pairs. In Fig. 12, two successive divisions of these two processes are compared.

COMBINATIONS OF GENES 61

The numerical results of meiosis, that is, the halving of the number of chromosomes, should not be allowed to eclipse even more important happenings. Suppose that, as in our example in an earlier chapter, a particular male carries, on one of his No. 1 chromosomes, the dominant gene, A, and on the other the recessive gene, a. His formula, then, might be written:

$$1^A\text{-}1^a \quad 2\text{-}2 \quad 3\text{-}3 \ldots 23\text{-}23$$

After several ordinary body-cell mitoses, the four resulting cells would be exactly like this original one, as in Fig. 12. At meiosis, however, he can put only one member of his pair No. 1 chromosomes into any one sperm. Therefore the sperm produced by the two special divisions would be of two kinds:

$$\text{either } 1^A \quad 2 \quad 3 \ldots 23$$
$$\text{or } 1^a \quad 2 \quad 3 \ldots 23$$

This is precisely the same thing that was dealt with in Chapter 2. The new complications, which will be considered now, arise when more than one gene is considered simultaneously.

Combinations of genes on different chromosomes

Let us suppose that the male we are discussing has, in addition to A and a on chromosome pair No. 1, another pair of genes, B and b, which are located on chromosome pair No. 2. We could write the formula for this male as follows:

$$1^A\text{-}1^a \quad 2^B\text{-}2^b \quad 3\text{-}3 \ldots 23\text{-}23$$

What happens when this male forms sperm? Each product gets only one member of each pair of chromosomes and it is wholly a matter of chance which of the two members of any one pair actually gets included into a given sperm cell. Suppose, in making a particular sperm cell, the 1^a member of the pair is the chosen one. Actually, the choice is quite like flipping a coin: the chance is one out of two that 1^a will be chosen. Now, during the formation of this same sperm, the same sort of decision has to be made for chromosome No. 2. This is again determined by chance, but it is quite independent of what happened with respect to the alternatives in chromosome 1. In this case, let us say that 2^b gets into the sperm we are talking about. Its composition, then, will be:

$$1^a \quad 2^b \quad 3 \ldots 23$$

But if the first decision had been for 1^A, then the resulting sperm would have been:

$$1^A \quad 2^b \quad 3 \quad 4 \quad 5 \quad 6 \ldots 23$$

Similar reasoning leads to the recognition of two more combinations:

$$1^a \quad 2^B \quad 3 \quad 4 \quad 5 \quad 6 \ldots 23$$

and

$$1^A \quad 2^B \quad 3 \quad 4 \quad 5 \quad 6 \ldots 23$$

In short, the combinations with respect to these two gene pairs that our male can transmit in his sperm consist of four types, AB, Ab, aB, and ab. The probability that any one sperm will have a particular one of these four combinations is one out of four.

The rest of the chromosomes have not been considered so far; our model could just as well have had only two pairs of chromosomes rather than 23. What happens, then, if chromosome Nos. 3, 4, 5, and so on also have a gene difference, which could be represented by Cc, Dd, Ee, etc.? Obviously, it gets harder and harder to figure out the number of combinations which might be expected to be produced, but the number is given by calculating the simple formula 2^n. Each chromosome pair has two alternatives; this explains why the base number is 2. The exponent, n, is the number of chromosome pairs. Thus, as we have seen in our two examples, $2^1 =$ two types, A and a; $2^2 =$ four types, AB, Ab, aB, and ab. For three pairs it would be 2^3, or eight; ABC, ABc, AbC, Abc, aBC, aBc, abC, and abc.

It should be noted here that if there is one difference on each chromosome, the formula calls for 2^{23} combinations, or 8,388,608. No two of these will be exactly alike from the genetic point of view. Although we have used the male as an example, the principle holds for the female as well. It is important to note, however, that a human female will produce only about 400 eggs in her lifetime. These will obviously be far fewer than the number of possible combinations. The principle is the same in card-playing. If one plays 400 games of bridge, the card hands received by the player represent only a small sample of the number of possible hands that might be dealt from the same deck of cards.[1]

Combinations of genes located on the same chromosome

That the genetic combination of genes possessed by one individual should be capable of more than eight million separate and distinct kinds of recombinations in the form of daughter cells seems remarkable enough. Yet this estimated number is based on oversimplified assumptions. It is likely that the number of possible combinations that might be formed is normally far greater than this.

The reason for this probable underestimation is that we have assumed that each chromosome has only one gene difference worthy of note. That is, we considered that chromosome No. 1, for instance, carried only one pair of genes, the members of which are different from one another. Very conservative estimates of the number of gene sites in a human cell indicate that there are about 10,000 present, thus chromosome No. 1, the longest in the set, would be expected to have at least 400 such sites whereas our calculations so far have dealt with differences at only one of these 400, represented by A and a.

Genes which are present on the same chromosome pair are said to be linked in their inheritance. Let us consider now the case of chromosome pair No. 1 in which there exist two gene differences, A and a and D and d. For the moment, we will leave the rest of the chromosomes out of consideration. For ease of exposition and visualization of the nature of the recombinations, it will be useful if the reader will visualize himself as the site of the recombinations.

Let us say, then, that your pair of chromosomes No. 1 may be represented in the following manner:

$$\underline{1} = \text{a b c d e f g h i j K l m n o p q r S t } \ldots \text{ z } \ldots$$

$$\overset{\bullet\bullet}{1} = \text{A b c D e f g h i j K l m n o p q r S t } \ldots \text{ z } \ldots$$

The underscored lineup of letters ($\underline{1}$) represents the single chromosome No. 1 which you received from your mother, whereas the alternate dotted one ($\overset{\bullet\bullet}{1}$) represents the chromosome No. 1 received from your father. Note that the 26 letters of the alphabet are quite insufficient to give even a rough idea of the 400 gene pairs which may exist on these two chromosomes.

The matter has been simplified by showing only two gene differences along the length of the two chromosomes. These differences are A and a and D and d. The chromosome received from your mother, then, contained the combination $\underline{\text{a}\quad\text{d}}$ (read as "small a, small d") whereas the one from your father had $\overset{\bullet\bullet\bullet\bullet\bullet\bullet\bullet}{\text{A}\quad\text{D}}$ (read as "large A, large D").

Now, when you in turn form reproductive cells, either the $\underline{\text{a}\quad\text{d}}$ combination which you got from your mother or the $\overset{\bullet\bullet\bullet\bullet\bullet\bullet}{\text{A}\quad\text{D}}$ combination which was originally from your father is very often passed on, intact, in the same combination in which you received them. But it is known that frequently the reproductive cell gets a combination that you yourself did not have, namely, A d or a D. This is accomplished by a process known as "crossing over."

Crossing over may be represented diagrammatically as follows. Before the time that the two members of each chromosome pair are separated and move into separate cells, they move very close together, with comparable regions adjacent to one another, thus:

```
 a  b  c  d  e  f    etc.
 ················
 A  b  c  D  e  f    etc.
```

While the chromosomes are closely associated like this, both of them duplicate their strands, so that the entire unit now consists of four, rather than two, as follows:

```
 a  b  c  d  e  f
 a  b  c  d  e  f
 ················
 A  b  c  D  e  f
 ················
 A  b  c  D  e  f
```

Now, two of these duplications will be maternal in origin (the solid lines) and two will be paternal. It frequently happens, however, that during or just after the duplication process, two of the four strands undergo an exchange of parts.

The exact mode of this exchange is not known but the result is simple enough. What has happened indicates that one paternal and one maternal strand have broken, probably simultaneously at the same point. The breaks heal up in a new way, so that two new strands are formed, each with part maternal (solid line) and part paternal (dotted line) material. When an event like this has occurred, let us say somewhere between the locus of b and d, the four strands may look like this:

a	b	c	d	e	f
a	b	c	d	e	f
A	b	c	D	e	f
A	b	c	D	e	f

This crucial stage can be recognized under the microscope (Fig. 13a). Each point where such an exchange has occurred is marked by an X-like crossing of strands, called a chiasma. Many such exchanges can occur in a single cell. After crossing over, the four strands of each chromosome are separated and are sorted out into separate cells. Any one of the four strands has an equal chance with the others of getting into a reproductive cell.

When straightened out and separated, after crossing over, the strands look diagrammatically like this:

a	b	c	d	e	f	g	h	...	z	...
a	b	c	D	e	f	g	h	...	z	...
A	b	c	d	e	f	g	h	...	z	...
A	b	c	D	e	f	g	h	...	z	...

Inspection of these strands will show that two of them (top and bottom) are identical to those which were received from your mother and father, respectively. If a particular reproductive cell gets one of these, the inheritance pattern would be the same, as we have seen previously. But the process has produced two "new" strands, which are made up of part maternal and part paternal material. Simply, the combinations derived from your parent were AD (from father) and ad (from mother). In the process of forming germ cells two new kinds have been gener-

COMBINATIONS OF GENES 67

ated: Ad and aD. Such recombinations are formed very frequently if the two genes concerned are far apart on the chromosome, and less frequently if they are close together.

Again, we should point out the sheer random nature of this process. The chromosome pairs can break and recombine at any

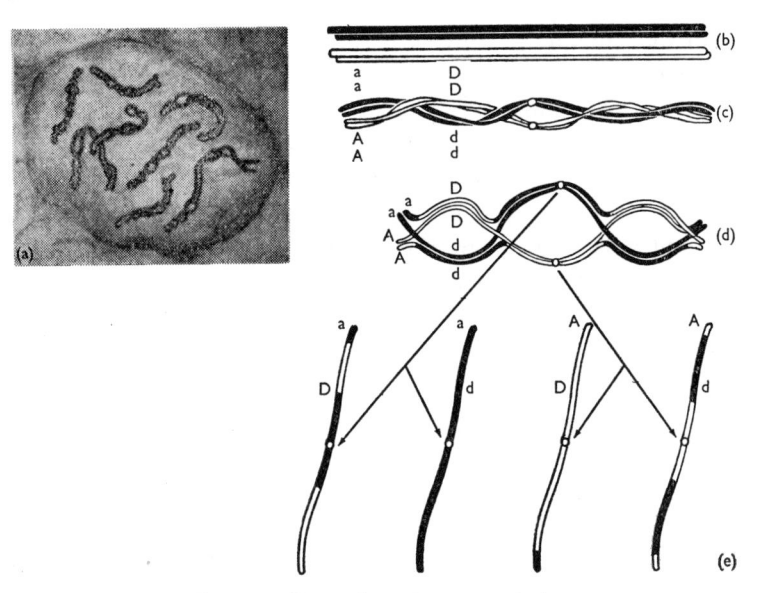

Fig. 13. Recombination at meiosis

(a) A drawing of an actual meiotic cell from a male; for clarity, only 8 of the 23 chromosome pairs are shown. Each unit consists of the maternal and paternal members of a pair of chromosomes (see Fig. 11) which have approached and twisted around each other [see (b) and (c); maternal-black, paternal-white]. (d) A diagram showing how, while together, crossing over of black and white occurs. The letters represent genes, as in the text explanation. When the two meiotic divisions follow (see Fig. 12), each of the four separate strands reaches a different sperm cell (e). As this happens independently for each of the 23 pairs, any one sperm gets a complex mixture of paternal and maternal genes. Events in the formation of the egg cell are similar; (a) is from plate 1, figure 2, A. E. Severinghaus, *Am. J. Anat.*, 70 [1942], 89; (b), (c), and (d) are from C. P. Swanson, *Cytology and Cytogenetics*, Englewood Cliffs, N.J., Prentice-Hall, Inc., 1957, pp. 285–86.

point along their length, and this is determined purely by chance, just as chance determines which of the four strands produced ultimately gets into a particular sperm or egg.

Potential recombining ability

In the example just given, it is obvious that any one chromosome can produce four different strands rather than two, as shown in the simple example. Assuming that two pairs of genes on each chromosome pair show differences (such as the Aa and Dd pairs show in the example above), the number of combinations when all the rest of the chromosome pairs are taken into account will be given by the formula 4^n, which in man will be 4^{23} or about 19 trillion (19,204,371,644,416).

If you have four children, your half contribution to each of them was drawn by chance from these combinations like four slips of paper, with numbers on them, might be drawn from an enormous vat containing all numbers from one up.

There is every reason to believe, however, that the number of combinations which are potentially possible is far greater than the numbers given so far. This is because of two further important facts which we shall consider now. These facts are: gene loci on a single chromosome number in the hundreds (we have said about 400 per chromosome) and the evidence is also very strong that the members of a pair of chromosomes, like your two chromosomes No. 1 from your mother and father, are likely to be different at a number of gene loci rather than just at two as we have assumed so far. If even so few as 2 percent of the gene sites showed differences, that is, about eight per chromosome, the number of possible combinations rises so high as to be quite beyond understanding. It is clear also that no man could live long enough to produce enough reproductive cells to be sure that all his possible combinations had been produced at least once. The actual number of reproductive cell combinations produced by an individual, even though numbering in the hundreds of millions, is never more than a minute fraction of the number that is possible.

We have considered so far that only a single crossing-over event occurs in the formation of a group, let us say, of four sperm. This is quite oversimplified, because examination of the chromosomes at the crucial time when they are paired and undergoing exchanges shows that they quite often show two or more exchanges per pair, and the frequency may run as high as five or even ten (see Fig. 13).

All this means that when you make a reproductive cell, the chromosomes that you got from your father and mother are probably never passed on intact by you to your children. You pass on chromosomes which represent various new and unique combinations of the genes which you got from your two parents. Most of these combinations never saw the light of day before and never will again, so great is the number and so low the probability for a particular combination to occur twice. Just as the sperm and egg from which you arose are truly unique productions of nature, so, when you reproduce, your half contribution to any particular one of your children is likewise unique.

Recombination at fertilization

Although the number of combinations discussed above is enormous, it by no means represents the ultimate. This is because the individual of the next generation arises not from one egg or sperm of one parent but from the chance union of two cells from two parents.

The process which goes on in the production of egg and sperm is roughly analogous to shuffling and dealing in card games. The gene combinations which may be produced by different meioses may be compared to the "hands." A single hand, dealt from one pack, however, corresponds only to the reproductive cell of one parent. The hereditary material of the fertilized egg arises through the union of two such recombined sets dealt from decks which were already quite different from one another before the dealing began.

Accordingly, it is obvious that the possibility of genetic variation is increased enormously by the final event of fertilization itself, which in effect combines cell products from two usually quite different hereditary lines.

In this final phase of gene recombination connected with sexual reproduction, chance again plays a dominant role. The union between the two cells, already having gene combinations which are chance drawings, is in itself the final crowning act of chance which determines the final genetic constitution of the new individual.

Gene recombination as just described has no connection with the ultimate origin of gene differences by the process of mutation. As in shuffling and dealing cards, the diverse gene patterns are present initially and are merely brought into new combinations at the time the reproductive cells are formed. In the analogy with card games, mutation might be likened to a change in one card, say a king of hearts, from a red to a purple color. All future decks which received duplications of this strange king might then form combinations which included it, but the actual formation of the new card, the mutation itself, is not in any way connected with the process of dealing.

Uniqueness of each human individual

The tremendous amount of inborn variation that is obvious between different persons is due to the fact that each individual begins as a unique combination of genes. Given even a moderate amount of chromosomal difference to begin with, the three phases of recombination are such that the probability of producing the same combination of genes twice is infinitely small. The initial variability of the human chromosomal material being very great, studies of gene recombination permit us to draw a conclusion of the utmost significance. This is that no two human individuals arising from two different fertilized eggs will be the same genetically. Not only do you, the reader, represent an absolutely unique combination existing on earth at this present time in human history, but there has never existed before, and will never exist again, the same combination that you represent. This quality of uniqueness lends dignity to each human being.

You got the details of your genetic endowment by the same processes that you might get a bridge hand. If the combination is good, you have been favored by good luck, purely and simply. If it is not, you are the victim of bad luck. No amount of propitiation of wrathful gods or wishful thinking has any effect on the random nature of genetic recombination.

To say that these recombination processes yield unrepeatable and unique combinations is not to say that some combinations do not closely resemble others. The fact that our children are different from us and from one another does not obscure the fact that they do resemble us and each other more than less closely related individuals. Family resemblance is based on the fact that the combinations are drawn from the same two parents and therefore are likely to have a greater similarity to each other than to combinations produced by a different line of human descent, such as that represented by the family next door. The explanation of the existence of differences between human groups, families, clans, and races and an assessment of their importance will be the subject of a later discussion. Just now, we must continue to try to understand differences between individuals in more detail because this is basic to going further.

Summary

You, as an individual, have a double set of chromosomes—23 pairs. One member of each of the 23 pairs came from your father, the other from your mother. When you form a reproductive cell (egg or sperm) you pass into it only one member of each pair. This cell will ultimately derive half of its genes from your father's chromosomes and half from your mother's. Assortment is wholly by chance and any given reproductive cell will contain contributions from both of your parents.

During reproductive cell formation, two processes provide for recombination of the genes on the chromosomes. First, there is the process of exchange of segments (crossing over) between the members of each pair of chromosomes. This recombines material from your father and mother so that a given chromosome going into the reproductive cell is a mosaic with parts derived from each of your parents. Second, these chromosomes which have been thus scrambled and recombined into new mosaics are, following this, independently assorted or dealt out from each of the 23 pairs of chromosomes. On some very conservative assumptions, you, as an individual, should be able to produce about 4^{23} genetically different kinds of reproductive cells. This is a very large number and it is probable that no two will be alike. These combinations are formed by wholly chance processes and are not related to the process whereby differences arise in the first place, namely, gene mutation.

When one reproductive cell joins in fertilization with one produced by similar processes by a person of the opposite sex, this new individual has a combination of genes unique in the history of human beings both past, present, and future. Thus no two individuals coming from different fertilized eggs are ever identical genetically. Recombination of preexisting small genetic differences carried in the chromosomes is far more important in explaining inborn differences than the occurrence of new mutations. The role of chance is dominant in all matters pertaining to the formation of the reproductive cells and there is no control possible over the chromosomal events responsible for recombination of genes.

Chapter 5

HEREDITY AND ENVIRONMENT

Separation of hereditary and environmental influences

SOMETIMES we ask meaningless questions and then add to our confusion in trying to answer them. A commonly asked but meaningless question is: Which is more important in the life of the individual, heredity or environment? There are two things wrong with putting the question in this way. First, both are essential ingredients, so that it is like asking whether the recording itself (the hereditary material) is more important than the electronic machine on which it is played (environment) in the reproduction of a symphony. Alone and by itself, isolated in a test tube, DNA forms a rather sticky material which is formless to the naked eye. When permitted to live, that is, to direct the accumulation of materials about itself, only then may it express its potencies.

A few human traits, such as eye color or blood group, serve as examples of characters with very strong hereditary determination. The genes present in the fertilized egg direct the formation of a certain pigment as the eyes develop in the embryo, and this process is highly independent of outside factors. Eye color thus cannot be altered by simple changes in the environment such as drops in the eyes, a changed diet, exposure to sunlight, or moving to a new climate.

This situation tempts us to say: "Eye color is hereditary." If by this we mean that the outcome is strongly determined by the programmed information in the genes, this statement is correct enough. Yet, when read literally, the statement "eye color is hereditary" might cause us to forget that a character, as such, is never inherited. What is inherited are the genes, which represent the potentiality of the character to develop, not the character itself.

This consideration is very important because relatively few characters exist which are as resistant to environmental conditions as eye color. Eye color is in fact a kind of trap leading us to believe that hereditary influences in other characters are equally as profound. This is definitely not so. Most other gene-affected characters are likewise altered by external environmental influences as well as by genes. This brings us to the second mistake made by the naïve questioner who wants to know, in a general way: "Which is more important, heredity or environment." Influence of nature and nurture are indeed almost universal in the living person, but the influence of the two factors is not equal on all characters. Therefore it is essential that the question be asked separately for each specific individual characteristic, whether eye color, body weight, susceptibility to tuberculosis, or intelligence.

For the reasons given above, then, our discussion will take one character at a time. Thickness of hair shows little effect of environment under any circumstances and its relationships appear to be quite like those of eye color. Degree of curliness, however, is in a somewhat different category because the final result is easy to alter artificially. As it emerges from the follicles, hair form shows a high degree of genetic determination; special diets or sudden frights have no effect on it. As soon as it grows long enough, wave-producing chemicals or curling irons, that is, environmental agents, can alter the character drastically. Without close inspection, one cannot be sure whether the curly hair one sees is primarily caused by the genes or an environmental agent or both. Such easy alteration of a character which has basically a high degree of genetic determination, and the concealment that goes with it, complicates the job of the human geneticist in separating hereditary and environmental influences.

Hair color, quite obviously, is in much the same category. Again, the color cannot be changed until it has grown out of the hair follicle, but once out the possibilities presented by human invention seem endless. Not all bleaching of hair, however, occurs under direct human influence. Let us suppose that two persons have identical, genetically determined hair colors. One may go about his daily work hatless in brilliant sunshine. This may result in the bleaching of his hair pigments to a much lighter shade than that which grows from the follicles themselves. The other individual, however, may be a miner and go daily, perhaps wearing a cap, into the dark of the mine. The hair color of the two will be quite different. In this case, the difference between the two will be due entirely to differences in their environmental way of life.

Skin color represents another superficial character. It depends on the deposition of the pigment melanin in the skin. In the presence of certain genes, heavy deposition of this pigment may begin long before birth in the early embryonic stages and continue throughout life. Depending on the number and action of the genes which are present, the resulting skin may be a very rich black or almost any intermediate shade to quite light. Even the lightest skins, however, contain quite a lot of the same kind of pigment that is present in the blackest; the difference is one of amount, not kind. Although there appears to be no way that a dark skin can be lightened, many light skins will change strikingly under the influence of ultraviolet rays, that is, the skin becomes sunburned. This is a good example of the participation of both heredity and environment in the final expression of a given character.

To begin with such traits as the above is perhaps helpful to the nonbiologist because he can see and appreciate the results in himself and his own family. It turns out, however, that human inheritance can be most easily studied with respect to certain specific chemical characteristics. Examples are the serum proteins which constitute the different blood groups, the types of hemoglobin or certain chemical by-products which appear in urine, because of a certain inherited mode of body chemistry. In the case of these conditions, a very simple test of body fluids is usually sufficient to identify the protein directly and, therefore, the presence of the gene which stands directly behind the protein in the body cells. These chemical characteristics are especially useful in human genetics, because, like the above example of eye color, their expression is not easily altered by the environment.

Just because a character is easy to measure and because we can ascertain rather easily that it has a strong hereditary basis does not automatically make it a particularly important character for the life of the individual or from the point of view of human understanding. Inheritance of hair and eye color are intrinsically interesting but their importance is principally as straws to show how the wind blows. Quite frankly, what we really would like to know is the role of heredity and environment in important human characters, such as disease, behavior, mental characteristics, and intelligence.

Most of the traits that have been discussed so far appear to have a relatively simple hereditary basis, that is, there are no more than three or four major gene pairs involved in the differences that we have discussed. The mode of inheritance can be at least partly determined by the analysis of pedigrees of families. This method of analysis is very limited, however, because human marriages are under absolutely no obligation to be of the kind we would like to have for analysis, and the family sizes are almost always much too small to reveal with statistical accuracy the types of genes which are acting. It should be remembered that most genetic analysis has depended on the property that genes have of being reassorted. Ideally, it is easiest to follow them from a parental cross through brother-sister matings to the second filial generation, a breeding system which does not occur in man, except in most unusual circumstances.

Attempts to assess the relative importance of heredity and environment run into many difficulties when we attempt to deal with characters which have both a complex hereditary basis and are also strongly affected by the environment. As we have said, disease conditions and behavior characteristics are perhaps the two categories that we would like to know the most about.

Let us see, by taking an example, just how modern genetic methods may be brought to bear on this problem. Let us say that you, as an individual, develop the disease diabetes. The basic trouble with you is that your pancreas is making insufficient insulin for the proper metabolism, that is, use of the sugars in your food. Now, if you diet very rigidly, avoiding all sugar, the symptoms of the disease will be less severe. In this sense, we may say that the condition is environmentally caused; if you do not eat sugar, you do not get the disease. Your brother, however, eats all the sugar he wants without developing diabetes; thus sugar is not the causative agent of the condition except under the particular genetic condition which leads, in you and other diabetics, to an improperly functioning pancreas. It is possible to show, by analysis of families showing diabetes, that one gene or at most a relatively small number of genes are responsible for the basic pancreatic abnormality. Yet, again, we cannot say that this hereditary factor will, in every instance, produce the disease. Some persons, having a pancreatic insufficiency, can nonetheless tolerate small amounts of sugar in the diet without signs of illness. If, however, such a person starts drinking beer or eating candy in large quantities, the condition develops.

In brief, diabetes is not "due to heredity" or "due to environment" in the way the statement is often naïvely made. It is due to the interaction between the two. Both hereditary and environmental criteria must be fulfilled before the condition develops. You must have the gene and you must eat sugar.

One of the aims of the human geneticist is to measure the relative contributions of heredity and environment for each of the human characteristics that are considered important. How many people who have a genetic predisposition to develop diabetes actually have such a low intake of sugar that they never develop the disease? To what extent can careful dietary control serve to suppress the appearance of the disease? Such studies, it should be emphasized repeatedly, must be done separately for each character. To take another example: The existence of a genetic blueprint which is prone specifically to the development of a type of skin cancer is well known. Exposure to the ultraviolet rays of the sun irritates the skin of such genetically sensitive persons, resulting in cancerous growths. Sun-bathing for persons having this rare condition is a dangerous matter. The resulting condition is thus produced by the interaction of hereditary and environmental influences.

To recognize that both heredity and environment are important in a myriad of human traits is not enough. Ideally, we want a measure of the relative strength of the two influences. This represents an enormously difficult problem and one which cannot be attacked by simple everyday observations, no matter how acutely they are made. Every parent makes observations on his own and neighboring children every day of his life. Such a small sample, however, viewed with unavoidable emotional bias, yields very few and very untrustworthy observations. These are the breeding grounds of unjustified and erroneous conclusions.

Take, for example, the elusive trait that we call personality. Two children of the same sex raised in the same house by the same parents, who try to provide the same conditions, often (in fact, usually!) develop quite different personalities. When one of these personalities is less desirable from the parents' point of view, some parents will say: "Oh well, Jimmy is just *different*," and proceed to cite observations which support this idea. By this they mean to ascribe the difference to heredity, overlooking the fact that Jimmy, if he is the older, may have developed an all-pervading jealousy of his younger brother. Environments of two children never can be exactly the same, even if they are contemporary in age and sex, as in some types of twins. Another set of parents might react by collecting all observations which support their idea that Jimmy really would be the same light-hearted extrovert as Johnny, if only somehow the environments which "produced" Johnny could be recreated for Jimmy.

In both cases, the mistake of oversimplification is made; it often leads to drastic measures of correction which are based on an incomplete understanding of the condition that is being treated. To treat properly, we must know how much of the condition is basically conditioned by heredity and how much by environment.

Study of human behavior is no place for the amateur. Psychologists who devote themselves to observations of behavior of human beings under various life conditions are better off than parents because they are able to observe impartially large numbers of people and are thereby able to assess the importance of the environment for certain specific types of behavior. Even in technical circles, however, the realization that each individual studied has an absolutely unique heredity has been slow. That there is a large hereditary ingredient in the structure and configuration of people's brains needs to be more widely realized. Much as we would like to believe that every person begins life with a closely similar or identical mental hereditary endowment, this is definitely not so. If no two human faces are alike because of gene recombination, then indeed there are no two brains alike either.

Studies of twins

Can we clarify the influences of heredity and environment, character by character? One way would be to create an absolutely uniform environment and then raise our various genetic types in this environment. Any differences which we observed would be due to the differences in heredity. It is, of course, absurd to suppose that such a method could be used in the study of human beings. In fact, it is difficult to approximate under even the best laboratory conditions.

The second way to separate hereditary and environmental influences is to somehow obtain cases where heredity is identical and then see how these genetic identities are affected by different environments. Although this might be thought to be as unattainable as the first set of conditions, it is a remarkable stroke of luck that nature does indeed provide genetic identities. Thus, so-called identical twins provide just the instance of genetic identity that we need for comparisons of this sort. Identical twins are individuals who both arose from the same fertilized egg, therefore the same unfertilized egg nucleus and the same individual sperm cell were basic to the formation of both of them. Identical twins result from the separation of the developing embryo into two parts very early in the development of the fertilized egg. The two groups of cells, which have become separated by some chance process not yet exactly understood, then are capable of developing into two complete and perfect individuals which have had exactly the same hereditary endowment from the very beginning.

Identical twins, sometimes called "one-egg" twins, must be distinguished from a second type of twinning in which the two members arise from the more or less simultaneous production, separate fertilization, and implantation in the uterus of two eggs at one time. In two-egg twins, the members of the pair will show no closer genetic relationship than any two children in the same family born at different times.

Identical twins are breath-takingly similar to one another. This similarity is roughly apparent at a glance but the depth of it can only be appreciated when careful measurements are made. In the first place, one-egg twins are always the same in sex, basic hair color and form, eye color, blood group, hemoglobin type, and many other features. This invariable similarity involves, of course, those characteristics the final form of which is strongly determined by genes. These facts themselves are of course of great interest, but in many characters identical twins differ somewhat from one another. As these are often characters of importance, we wish to know the degree of environmental influence on these characters.

As identical twins provide unique cases of genetic identity, it would seem at first glance that any difference between two such persons, in any character, could be safely ascribed to the influence of the environment. This is essentially true but there is a possible pitfall here. Identical twins raised together in a home tend to have environments which are more similar than children of like sex raised a few years apart in the same home. Early attempts to get around this difficulty made special use for study of pairs of identical twins which for some reason had been separated at an early time and were subsequently reared apart from one another. Such cases are, of course, hard to find and are relatively rare compared with the number of cases in which twins are reared in the same home. Nevertheless, enough cases have been found for an extensive analysis. The results reveal that in such things as physical appearance, stature, and body build such twins are strikingly similar even if raised under quite different conditions.

The very great stumbling block in such studies, however, is

providing a basis for comparison of environments. How does one compare two human environments, including measuring all the essential features of, for example, love, security, educational opportunity, cultural attitudes of parents, accidental occurrences, and associations inside and outside of the family, to mention only a few?

A more fruitful kind of comparison is as follows. The degree of similarity between two individuals arising from one egg, which are always of the same sex, is determined by measurement. For each set of one-egg twins, a nonidentical, two-egg pair, which happen to be of the same sex, are simultaneously studied. If environment tends to make the two members of any twin pair similar to one another, the effect should be the same on both types of twins. If identicals on the average are more similar to one another than comparable pairs of two-egg twins, this gives a quite meaningful estimate of the strength of hereditary determination of the character which is being measured.

Roles of heredity and environment in specific characters
Some human physical traits

Let us begin with the standing height of an individual and use this character as an example of how twin analysis can clarify the roles of heredity and environment. Measurement of a large number of one-egg twin pairs shows that the average difference in height is a little more than half an inch (two centimeters) even among twins reared apart (Fig. 14). What does this mean? In the first place, the fact that two individuals with identical heredity are different in height at all means that there is some environmental influence. Taken alone, however, the fact that identical twins differ by half an inch is not very informative about the strength of heredity in this character. This fact does acquire significance, however, when we compare this half-inch figure with the difference in height between comparable pairs of two-egg twins. This difference averages nearly an inch and a half, about two and a half times as much as the difference between identicals. Sibs, that is, ordinary brothers or ordinary sisters in this case, do not differ from two-egg twins in this trait. We may say, then, that heredity plays a slightly larger

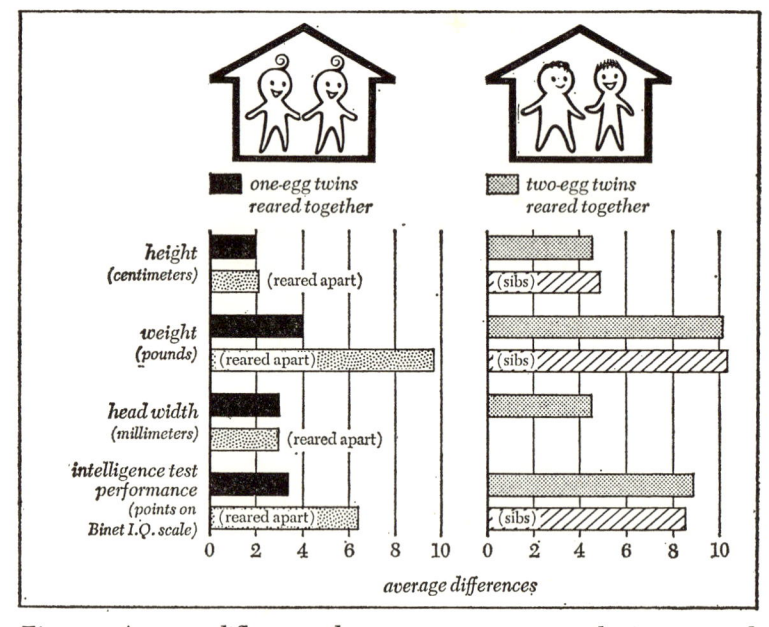

Fig. 14. Average differences between one-egg twins (left) compared with those between like-sexed two-egg twins (right)

Comparisons involving twins reared together and sibs (two ordinary brothers or two ordinary sisters) are based on measurements made on 50 or more twin pairs in each category. Measurements on one-egg twins reared apart are based on 20 pairs. The existence of differences between one-egg twins (which have the same genotype) shows a role of environment in all four traits. That all differences are larger among two-egg twins proves a role for heredity in all four traits. Weight and intelligence-test performance are more easily modified by environment than height and head width.

role in the determination of height than does environment. A good diet, however, will help to stretch the performance of the genes to their maximum.

The usefulness of information on identical twins reared apart is apparent from the figures on body weight (Fig. 14). Identical twins differ by about four pounds and nonidenticals by about ten among pairs of twins reared in the same home. Identical twins reared apart, however, show nearly a ten-pound difference. We may conclude that weight is a character which is capable of being strongly modified by the environment, but with nonetheless a smaller role which can be ascribed to heredity.

The special kind of information provided by the study of twins has been obtained for a very large number of human characteristics. Each character shows its own particular combination of the influences of heredity and environment and it is often difficult to predict from uncritical observations which influence will be stronger.

One of the advantages of the twin method is that it can be used without regard to the complexity of the hereditary basis. In other words, although the method does not permit us to specify the number of genes involved or their mode of inheritance, we can still make a very useful estimate of the role of heredity. Thus, all sorts of characters which would be very difficult to follow in the analysis of pedigrees can be investigated in twins and the results are often quite surprising. The two members of a twin pair often get the same infectious diseases, such as, for instance, tuberculosis. Now tuberculosis is a disease which is "caused" by a bacterium, a definite environmental agent. But from the study of identical and nonidentical twins it is suggested that some gene combinations are more likely to be susceptible to serious attacks by this bacterium than others. How strong is this tendency?

Cases are assembled of identical twins in which at least one twin is affected with tuberculosis. We then ask the question: How often are members of a twin pair affected by the disease? We can express this in terms of the percent of twin pairs studied which show similarity. The most extensive studies show that

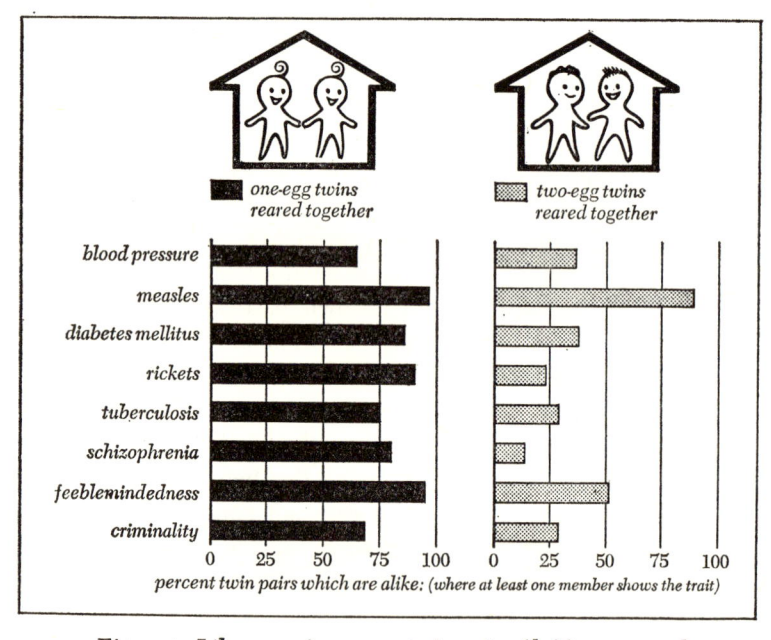

Fig. 15. Likeness of one-egg twin pairs (left) compared with two-egg twin pairs (right), for cases where at least one member shows the trait

In every case, one-egg twins show a higher percent of twin pairs alike. This proves that hereditary susceptibilities play a role even in such environmentally "caused" conditions as measles, tuberculosis, and criminality.

in about 74 percent of such identical twin pairs both members contract active tuberculosis (Fig. 15). This fact standing by itself tells us nothing about the existence of a hereditary basis for tuberculosis. Two children of like age and sex raised in the same home with the same parents might be expected to show a great deal of similarity in the infectious diseases which they contract.

The real significance of this percentage figure for identical twins is brought out when it is compared with information for two-egg twins of the same sex. In this case, such nonidentical twins both develop tuberculosis in only about 28 out of a hundred such twin pairs (Fig. 15). Nonidentical twins, like identicals, are reared together and on the whole should have environments which are very similar to those of identical twins. The existence of a marked difference between the two types of twins proves that hereditary factors play an important role in determining whether or not a given individual will develop tuberculosis. To be diseased, it is obvious that an individual must come in contact with the bacterium, but some individuals have hereditary constitutions which make them more resistant to infection than others. The disease results from the interaction of both hereditary and environmental factors. Neither one, in this case, can be said to play the dominant role.

A vitamin has sometimes been called something that will make you sick if you don't eat it. It is a substance that must be in the diet; otherwise, a disease, caused by a deficiency of the vitamin, will develop. Rickets, for example, is "caused" by a deficiency of vitamin D. As in the case of tuberculosis, a superficial view of the situation would assign no role to heredity in the causation of the disease. In tuberculosis, disease arises because of the irritations, poisonous substances, and invasions of a specific bacterium, the tubercle. In the other, disease arises because of a specific nutritional lack, that is, vitamin D is insufficient in the diet. But when rickets is examined in identical and nonidentical twins, we find that identical twins are the same in 88 percent of twin pairs studied whereas for two-egg twins the comparable figure is only 22 percent (Fig. 15). Evidently, there is a genetic proneness which in the case of individuals with certain genes or combinations of genes makes those individuals more susceptible to shortages of this particular vitamin. A teaspoonful of cod-liver oil does not have the same effect on every individual.

The two cases above have been selected for the discussion of the heredity-environment interplay because they appear, on the superficial view, to be easily "ascribable to environment" and thus "could not be hereditary." But now we see that both nature and nurture are intimately involved and that treatment and prevention of these conditions must take both factors into account. Both conditions "run in families." It is interesting that before the environmental agents necessary for the appearance of these conditions were discovered the error was on the other side. Rickets was at one time, before the discovery of vitamin D, considered to be "hereditary."

Some human mental traits

The time has now come to consider the interplay of heredity and environment on the appearance of mental traits. Although the tendency is to discuss this subject in terms of the development of acute mental and personality disorders, actually, variations in intelligence among normal persons represents a subject of far greater importance.

The uniqueness of the human species in nature involves first and foremost the brain. This organ is the seat of the behavior characteristics which give us our distinctive humanness. The brain dictates the difference between an individual who emanates warm human love and another who manifests fierce human ruthlessness. The capacity of the human brain for the building of culture goes so far beyond that of our nearest animal relatives that we must be wary of how far we can go in the interpretation of human behavior in the light of the studies on the lesser brains of other animals.

The brain of man is the prime instrument in nature for profiting by experience. Impressions are stored and are drawn on for years afterwards as conscious or unconscious guides to behavior. By its very nature, the brain lacks rigid determination. The forefoot of a mole is specifically predetermined and shaped by the genes to develop into a rigidly fixed functional shovel for the moving of quantities of earth in a burrow. It can do no more, nor can the mole brain learn to direct the use of this arm in any different manner. A human brain is born an open instrument, ready to begin immediately the recording of events that are and are not significant. The interaction of this organ with the stream of events that go through it, leaving their marks, provide the basis of the personality, the true individuality of the human being.

How can we measure the mental capacities of a human individual? Can we estimate, as we can in the physical trait of stature, the roles of heredity and environment in specific mental traits? Ingenious intelligence tests have been devised which attempt to provide a sort of over-all measure of this elusive and complex property which we call intelligence. Performance of these tests varies enormously from individual to individual over a great range. Despite optimistic claims, no sort of intelligence test provides an unequivocal measure of the hereditary ingredient of intelligence. As has been pointed out in previous paragraphs, almost every characteristically human action of the brain is conditioned by experience. This begins at the moment of birth. It is for this reason that intelligence tests devised by and for one cultural or ethnic group cannot be sensibly used for groups which from the very start subject the brains of their young to radically different influences. As in the case of physical traits, twin studies have given the most reliable information on the role of nature-nurture in the matter of intelligence.

Before examining the twin studies, however, mention should be made of the quite clear cases of major mental defects which have their principal bases in simple hereditary conditions. As pointed out previously, variations of intelligence in the normal range are far more important than the severe impairments, as far as the population of the world is concerned. On the other hand, the drastic effect which a small defect in heredity can have on a single individual must be recognized.

An example is the rare recessive gene for phenylketonuria. The result of two doses of this gene is an inborn error of metabolism which can be recognized by tests of the urine of the affected individual. The basic malfunction is the inability of the individual to metabolize the amino acid phenylalanine, a common constituent of a protein diet. Unmetabolized phenylalanine, as it accumulates in the body, can in turn affect the development of the brain, causing severe mental retardation. Fortunately, however, such individuals can be salvaged if, from birth, they are put on a phenylalanine-free diet.

In the case of the well-known and more common "rh" genes, protein differences dictated by them may, for some mother-fetus combinations, result in cross-immunity reactions. One conspicuous result of this incompatibility is massive destruction of the blood cells of the fetal child, so that often the child is born with a low blood count, that is, a severe anemia. Mental impairment frequently occurs because the anemic blood carries insufficient oxygen to the developing brain, which has rather large oxygen requirements. As accounted previously, the basic underlying genetic cause of mongolian idiocy is the imbalance due to the presence of an extra chromosome, although the pathways leading to brain damage are not known.

The roles of heredity and environment in mental defect are

clearly indicated by twin studies. Nearly 500 twin pairs have been examined in which at least one member was classified as feeble-minded. Among identical twins 94 percent of the pairs studied had both members affected, whereas among two-egg twins the comparable figure is only 47 percent (Fig. 15). Among individuals with identical hereditary materials, furthermore, the detailed type of mental defect frequently shows close correspondence, whereas among the nonidenticals no such correspondence is seen. These facts point to a very strong role of the hereditary blueprint in mental defectiveness.

In the above examples, the defect in brain function is present at birth. Some harmful genes and gene combinations, however, do not manifest themselves until much later in life. Because the person seems normal at birth and may remain within the normal range for many years prior to the onset of difficulty, the presence of hereditary influences does not suggest itself readily. This is especially so with regard to mental difficulties in which environmental tensions and stress appear to be the main force bringing on the trouble.

The mental disease called schizophrenia is an outstanding example. Onset usually does not occur until the individual is over 20 years of age. An hereditary ingredient in schizophrenia is suggested by the fact that the condition runs in families. Children of affected persons have the condition about 20 times more frequently than the general population. Family analyses suggest that possibly a single gene plays a major role in the condition with a relatively small number of other genes modifying the action of the main one. Twin studies confirm the existence of a strong hereditary basis. Among affected pairs of one-egg twins, 80 percent both show the condition, whereas the comparable figures for nonidentical twins is 13 percent (Fig. 15). The fact that identical twins do not always both come down with the condition confirms that nongenetic factors are also involved. Thus, onset is precipitated by emotional stress in much the same way that onset of diabetes is often precipitated by stress in the form of high intake of sugar. At the same time, it is equally clear that the basic nerve-cell patterns of the brain may indeed be so structured by the genes as to result in a personality which is especially susceptible to emotional shocks. At the lower levels of intelligence-test performance, in feeble-mindedness, for instance, it is not difficult to recognize a quite strong influence of heredity. The difficult problem remains of assessing the hereditary ingredient in determining the differences within the range of normal intelligence. High accomplishment in science, art, and indeed politics definitely runs in families, yet this kind of performance can be so strongly influenced by nongenetic factors within the family environment that one must be very cautious in making interpretations.

Twin studies show nonetheless that identical twins make more similar scores on intelligence tests than do two-egg twins (Fig. 14). The mean difference between identicals reared together is about three points on the Binet I.Q. scale; that of nonidenticals is between eight and nine. As in many other traits, the similarity of two-egg twins is close to that of sibs of like sex, showing that contemporary rearing and age similarity do not force twins into greater similarity. Intelligence, as measured by such tests, therefore shows a considerable hereditary ingredient. Studies of one-egg twins reared apart, however, are most interesting. As will be noted in Fig. 14, such twins vary twice as much as similar twins reared in the same home. As in the case of body weight, this indicates a large role for environment.

Surely it comes as no surprise that general intelligence, as measured in this way, can be strongly influenced by both heredity and environment. Intelligence is clearly not so rigidly dictated by the genes as are such things as eye color, basic skin and hair color, hair texture, and head width. Intelligence is a genetically conditioned character which is highly modifiable by environmental influence. In an over-all way, heredity and environment appear to play about equal roles (see Fig. 16).

Although single genes are the principal agents in some cases of feeble-mindedness, there is no evidence that superior per-

gene combinations affecting intelligence	ENVIRONMENT		
	poor	moderate	highly favorable
INFERIOR	F	D	C
AVERAGE	D	C'	B
SUPERIOR	C	B	A

Fig. 16. Heredity and environment in mental accomplishment

Excellent performance (A) by an individual who carries a superior gene combination can be normally expected only when a highly favorable environment is also supplied. Failure (F) of the individual to perform at a satisfactory level is likely where both the gene combination and the environment are of poor quality. Even a highly favorable environment cannot overcome a genetic deficiency, nor can genetically superior equipment guarantee success if environmental opportunity is lacking. Note: Head shape, used for diagrammatic purposes, probably has no relationship to the genetic basis of intelligence, nor is a good house the most important ingredient of the environment.

formance, at the genius level for instance, can be related to the effects of a single gene. The hereditary ingredients in genius seem more likely to be related to the chance formation of an unique combination of genes conferring certain mental properties.

Among the many characteristics of one-egg and two-egg twins

that have been investigated is the number of instances in which the members of the two types of twins both run into conflict with the law, that is, acquire a criminal record. In identical twin pairs where at least one had such a record, 68 percent of the pairs studied showed that both had criminal records.

Among nonidenticals of the same sex, only 28 percent are so involved (Fig. 15). It seems absurd to suggest that anyone is a born criminal; conflict with the law is a behavior pattern which can be shown to be strongly correlated with certain social conditions. Yet, the striking similarity of one-egg twins suggests again that certain hereditary blueprints of the brain result in greater susceptibility to stresses and temptations. This realization does not alter the fact that some environments elicit high incidences of crime nor does it provide an excuse for a culprit, who may be tempted to claim that he was "born that way" and can't help himself. These data function mainly in clarification; we must be warned not to oversimplify a problem as old as human society itself.

Receptiveness of the human brain to environmental influence

To try to represent the biological function of the human brain through analogies is certainly to invite failure. Perhaps, however, a vague idea may be conveyed by the following. A child's brain at birth is already essentially complete in its basic equipment. The brain has developed in the nine months before birth according to the blueprint contained in the genetic information. The brain is not a mass of raw materials at birth, as yet unorganized. Its essential elements are already assembled in particular patterns. Like an electronic computer which has not yet been supplied with power, its millions of nerve-fiber connections, fresh and new and as yet unused, are already complete and await only the impulses. Into the circuits are connected recording devices ready to begin recording information minute by minute, day by day, month by month, year by year. But recording is not all; there is correlation. All these devices must be interconnected, so that a recorded impression of ten years ago may instantaneously be brought into relationship with a present occurrence.

Thus far, so-called electronic "brains" can perform only the simplest of the functions of the human brain. Possibly, an electronic coordinating device might some day be built which approaches it more nearly. If so, however, even the poorest of human brains would be equivalent to an auditorium packed solid with electronic devices.

If no two brains are the same to begin with, it is also true that no two people, even if they are identical twins reared in the same family, have the same experiences. A person who has been stung by a bee thereafter behaves very differently towards bees than one who has yet to record this experience. However, we cannot overlook the possibility that brains of different conformation may correlate this information about bees quite differently. To illustrate with a hypothetical example: Being stung by a bee is a pretty traumatic experience for a child and his brain will usually record, that is, remember, many other things associated with the sting, such as the exact place, what persons were nearby, the kind of weather, and so on. As times goes by, most brains can soon separate the essential part, that is, that the insect itself is the culprit and is to be avoided in the future. Other brains may be slower to do this; they might form a permanent association between bee stings and being outdoors, or with sunny days or with Uncle John because he was present at the time. Even all men might be blamed, because Uncle John was a man. Brains vary in their capacity to interpret the environment, and these capacities are very likely to have large inborn ingredients. This is essentially what we mean by intelligence.

Certain ingredients of human behavior are to be found in lower animals, yet man has basic features which are human and human alone. Consider the way a man would escape from a predatory animal such as a lion compared with the way a zebra escapes. The latter is served by fixed adaptive features, its keen sense of smell, fleetness of foot, large unwieldy size, and curious stripes, which serve as disruptive camouflage. All of these features are largely fixed in the zebra's heredity. It escapes without cunning, reflection, or thought; the zebra brain is only able to serve the proper functioning of these unvarying protective devices.

Man is neither fast enough nor large enough, nor properly colored, to escape by such means. When threatened, his brain works; he thinks of a way out. Into his mind crowd with incredible rapidity a series of observations he has made since birth, all that he has learned in a lifetime of intelligent action. Most likely he will shoot the lion with an instrument which he carried because experience has taught him the danger of the unarmed condition; he may go to a place of safety which he has previously noted as a haven in an emergency. He may even, through his knowledge of the lion's relatively stereotyped behavior, be able to double his trail, to trick the lion into stalking a dummy position, while he moves safely off in the opposite direction. Adaptable behavior fits the action to the particular occasion. Man has no substitute for learning by individual experience.

Not all men, however, have brains which are equally able to perform these wonderful feats of sensory perception, storage, and coordination. Whereas every person has one of these master instruments, they differ in basic quality. The details of the construction of each brain vary according to the instructions contained in the genetic blueprint. There may be differences in the fidelity of the organs of perception or in the delicacy of their coordination. Certain areas may be present but only poorly connected to other areas; the opportunities for basic variation in a structure of this complexity are enormous.

More than any other human characteristic, mental capacity unites the influences of heredity and environment in a most intimate and detailed way. Almost every action or behavior pattern of an adult is environmentally conditioned in the sense that experience with the environment played a role in determining it. But if the instrument on which the recording was made distorted or blurred the original experience, future actions with regard to previous experience may be curious, unpredictable, confused, fearful, antisocial, or any one of a long series of unsavory possibilities. Desirable mental qualities may be locked up by emotional difficulties, themselves of complex origin. Children start learning at an extraordinarily early age. Some cultures expose children to training along intellectual lines at the earliest possible moment, in others a great value is placed on other things, on social relationships, on love, respect, and cooperation.

In the modern world, the achievements of science, engineering, and mathematics stand, for better or for worse, at the center of the stage. Quite rightly we expend enormous efforts to apply the best in schooling to the best of brains. We should not make the mistake, when we encourage these capacities, of attaching supreme values to intellectual achievement. High intelligence often does, but does not necessarily, carry with it a warmth of human understanding, a sensitivity to the enduring values of life, a tolerance and love of the human species, the ability to accept that paradox of vice and virtue as one's own.

Just as we should not attempt to argue that all human difficulties arise from hereditary differences in brains, so we must also guard against the opposite view, which would contend that we can force every brain into a mold. Even if we could agree on a desirable paragon of virtue, no environmental influence could be strong enough to produce it. Every brain and every personality, however, no matter how deviant into criminality, how emotionally disturbed, or how initially retarded gains from good educational practice, the strongest environmental force for good which we possess.

Summary

No final resulting character is "purely hereditary." What is inherited is a series of determining genes. Genes must react with and operate through the environment to produce the character. Characters are not inherited, only genes are. The character is always the outcome of two forces, the nature of the determining genes and the environment in which this genetic information finds itself.

The strength of hereditary determinancy as opposed to environmental influence depends on the specific character itself. Each character must be considered separately. Eye color, for example, shows strong adherence to the dictates of the hereditary particles. Skin color adheres less rigidly because if lightly pigmented it can be darkened by the environmental influence of the sun. Some abnormal genes or gene combinations cause major effects even in the presence of the best environment that can be provided. Such are the abnormalities in blood proteins, in the development of brain or bone or muscle. Susceptibility to diabetes, rickets, tuberculosis, or to cancer or a large number of other important conditions have differing strengths of predisposing heredity. It is no longer valid to dismiss tuberculosis as "due to infection with an environmental agent, the tubercle bacillus." In some genetically resistant individuals, infection may occur without noticeable effect; conversely, individuals with hereditary susceptibilities may require treatment (i.e., environmental manipulation) to prevent disease.

Twin studies in particular have revealed with clarity the relative roles of heredity and environment in many human normal and abnormal traits, including the delicate and subtle differences in human brains. The latter form the basis both for behavior which is generally considered good and that which is generally considered bad. The human brain is an instrument which preceives and records environmental influences. Its mode of operation is through the correlation of these environmental influences; this is what makes it unique in nature. Yet hereditary configurations dictate the norms of operation of this instrument. It is so complex that small defects in cell associations, likened to wiring in an electronic computer, may result in distortion of received messages. The result may be that such a brain functions badly, whereas another functions well when it receives the same environmental impressions.

Initial inequalities of mental equipment provide at least a partial explanation for the enormous variability of so-called normal individuals when faced with intelligence tests. The human brain has many highly desirable characteristics not necessarily correlated with the higher degrees of intelligence. We must guard against trying to guide our education with respect to only the most superior of human brains. Education cannot force every individual into the same mold, no matter how perfect the environment. Education is a major force for good, but in the face of enormous genetic diversity we cannot expect the miracle of a universal panacea.

Chapter 6

THE INDIVIDUAL AND
HIS GROUP

UP to this point, the discussion has dealt with individuals. The gene combination which you carry has never seen the light of day before and will never occur again. It is unique in nature. Yet no man is an island unto himself, even in the strictest biological terms. Although physically separate, he is part of a group with which he shares genes because of common descent. Kinship, that is, genetic relationship, is closest and most easily discernible in the case of his immediate family. When relationship is less close, second cousins, for example, the mind can no longer understand it easily. Despite this, relationship between second cousins is a close one from the genetic point of view. Complicating the matter, furthermore, is the fact that the uniqueness of the individual in most cases tends to override superficial family resemblances to such an extent that even individuals as closely related as two brothers are often difficult to recognize as such.

The statement is often made that two persons, families, or larger groups are "not related." By this is meant that the speaker does not know what the degree of relationship is. As a matter of actual fact, however, you who read these words, no matter what your line of descent, are related to me, the writer of them.

Persons who have become intrigued with their own ancestry and have attempted to work out the genealogy of their families are aware of the enormous complexity of the job. Even the most persistent researcher finds that the mathematical progressions and intricacies of cross relationships force him to abandon the job only a few generations back. If the simplification of using yourself may be permitted, your genes came from recombinations of two genotypes, those of your parents. These two persons, in turn, derived their gene combinations from your four grandparents, and these from your eight great-grandparents, and so on. In Fig. 17 is given a diagram of this expansion which extends back six generations. Of the 64 individuals in the earliest generation, each, on the average, makes an equal contribution to your heredity. This point seems worth stressing when discussing genetics, because in genealogy it is customary to simplify matters by tracing back only along a few lines of descent, usually those bearing the family surname or leading back to some famous person. Each line of descent has an equal chance to be important from the genetic point of view.

In constructing such a diagram as Fig. 17, an important oversimplification has been made; it has been assumed that none of these ancestors are related to one another. If one were to continue with this assumption and expand the diagram back for only 30 generations (about a thousand years) the calculation shows that you would have had around a billion ancestors just in that generation alone. This number is probably greater than the population of the entire world 1,000 years ago, so if the calculation was made for the rest of the individuals now alive, the number of ancestors involved would be astronomical in size and the whole exercise quite absurd.

There are two reasons why the above calculations lead to this absurdity. In the first place, when there is a relationship between forebearers, one "loses" ancestors. For example, if two of your great-grandparents had the same parents, this would mean that two of your four grandparents would have been cousins. The effect of this minor degree of relationship would be to reduce

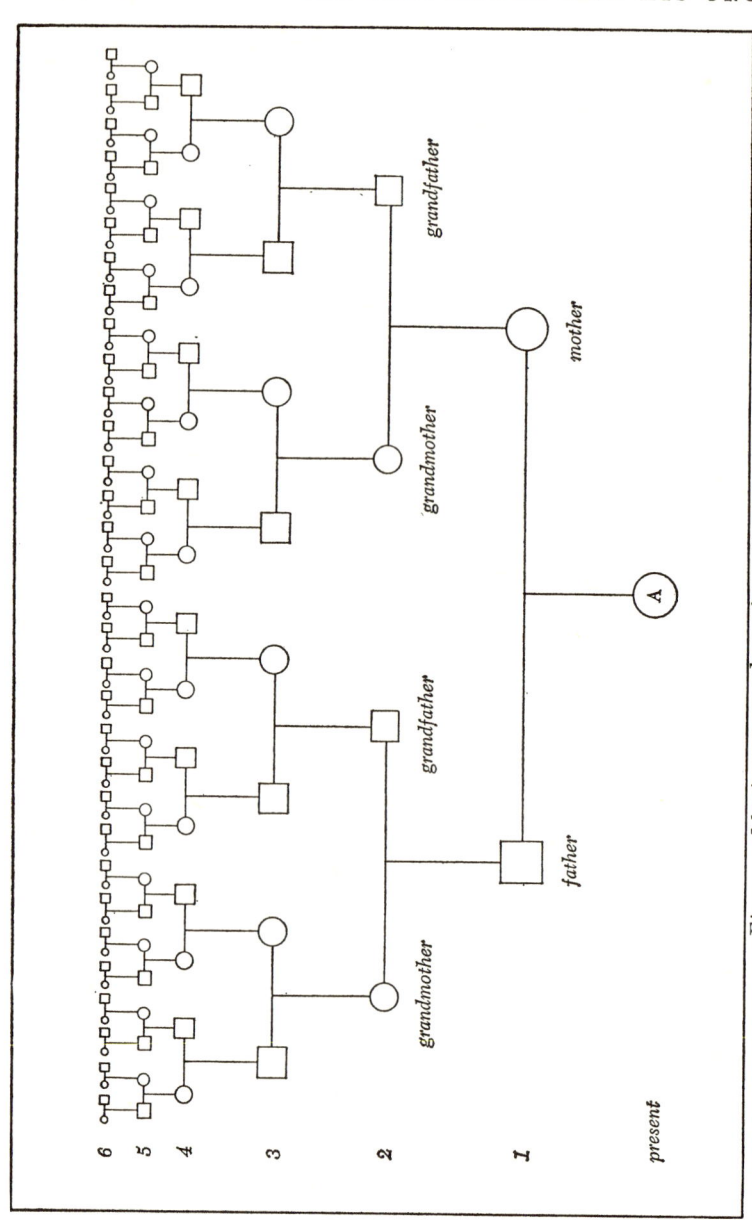

102   THE INDIVIDUAL AND HIS GROUP

Fig. 17. Maximum number of ancestors in six generations

The ancestry of one person (A) is given. Squares are males and circles are
females. The total number of ancestors in the six generations is 126.

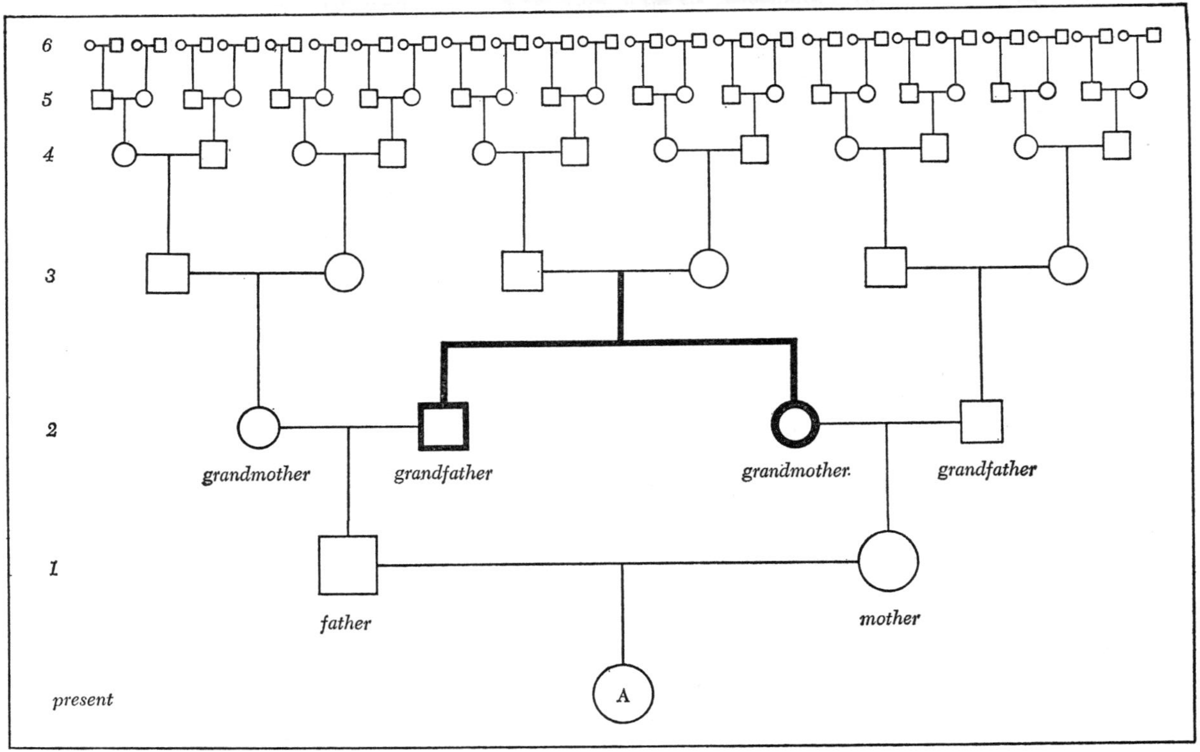

Fig. 18. "Loss of ancestors" due to relationship between some of them

The parents of A are first cousins. Thus two of his grandparents (on opposite sides of his family) are brother-sister (shown in bold lines, center of figure). Because of this, A has only six rather than eight great-grandparents (compare generation 3 with the same line in Fig. 17). The total number of ancestors in six generations is 96 rather than 126.

the number of ancestors in your six-generation pedigree from 126 to 112, a "loss" of 14 ancestors. This is shown in Fig. 18.

Not only is the maximum number of ancestors that a living person can theoretically have inevitably reduced by relationships among these ancestors, but persons now living of necessity share many of the same ancestors. Thus, as one follows the expansion diagrams back for a number of individuals of an existing population, even seemingly unrelated persons can be seen to have diagrams which are bridged and overlapped only a relatively small number of generations back. In this sense, our families are larger than we think. Indeed, sooner or later, every human being is related through this process of ancestor-sharing. The brotherhood of man is a noble ethical concept but it is a great deal more than that: it is a scientific reality as well.

The human gene pool

The individuals which make up the existing population of the world are, then, related by descent. Some groups, however, such as groupings of individuals according to our traditional family concepts, are made up of relatively closely related individuals and it is convenient, in examining populations, to start at the family level.

Let us begin the discussion of populations by imagining the following situation. A small island in the South Pacific, let us say about 40 square miles, has on it a population which consists of 100 persons of reproductive age (Fig. 19b). The island is small but has food resources sufficient to support the population well. The people live in a single integrated community without subdivision into separate isolated villages. Possible future changes are diagrammed in Figs. 19c and 19d; these will be considered later. Let us further assume that all persons on the island are the descendants of an original pioneer family of six persons which

THE INDIVIDUAL AND HIS GROUP 105

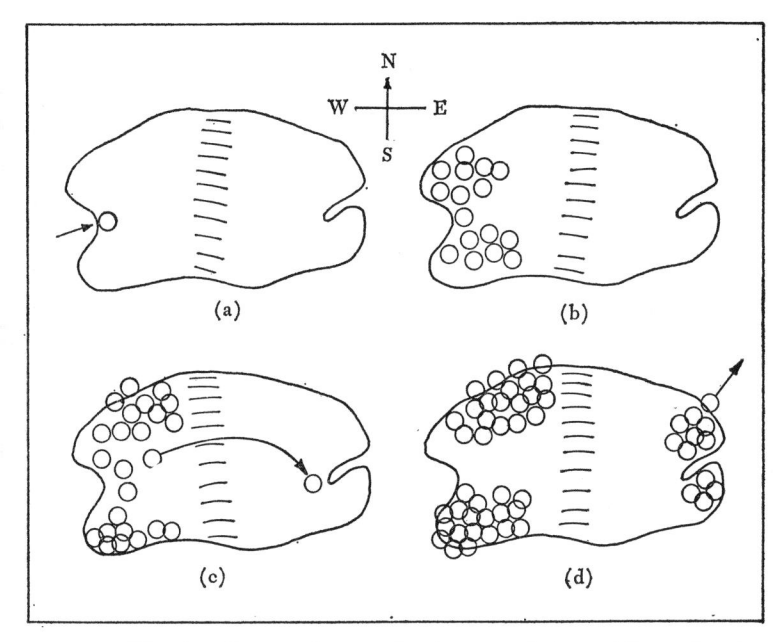

Fig. 19. The founding and growth of a population with tendencies towards inbreeding and isolation

(a) Island colonized from the west by one couple with four children. Close inbreeding will be obligatory in the founding of the population if there are no more migrants. (b) Small population of 100 persons derived from (a) about four generations (120 years) later. There have been no new migrants. The population consists of 16 families living in one integrated village in which intermarriage occurs freely, forming a single gene pool. (c) Same island a few generations later. The west village is larger and partially divided into north and south districts. One family has migrated over the mountains to the east. Genetic variability among the islanders tends to be low, compared with that which would be found in Fig. 20b. (d) Island now has two major villages each of which has two partially isolated communities. Intermarriage between persons from these different isolated areas is restricted, so that the gene pool of the island population is effectively subdivided. Emigrants from the island could perpetuate the tendencies shown in these diagrams. Within each gene pool, genetic variability tends to be low, but differences may become established between them.

landed on the island about four generations (120 years) previously (Fig. 19a). There have been no immigrants since that time.

Under these rather diagrammatic circumstances, it is easy to see that these 100 people are united by a very strong biological bond, a bond of common heredity. But just what does "common heredity" mean in this case? What, indeed, is it that a large number of genotypes, each different from the next due to genetic recombination, can be said to have in common? From the mathematical point of view, the population of the island has a corporate heredity, a gene pool. It is a pool in the same sense that a business syndicate represents the pooled resources of its members. The genes, brought in by the original family, are the genetic resources. The population, therefore, represents a pool of genes; each individual shares in that pool because he himself represents a chance drawing of genes out of the pool. The gene pool is the biological bond that unites the individuals. Their genes were drawn from it when they were formed and when they marry and have children they will in turn contribute to it and function to perpetuate it.

In order to visualize the way in which the individual is related to the gene pool, let us take a precise example. Each of the 100 young adult persons on the island has a pair of gene loci which have to do with blood groups. Persons with the genotype $I^A I^A$ have in their cells a mucopolysaccharide called "A," that is, they have the A blood group. A person who has these two gene loci both occupied by B, that is, who is $I^B I^B$, shows the "B" mucopolysaccharide. A person who carries one of each, that is, $I^A I^B$, has both mucopolysaccharides and is designated blood group "AB." By a simple blood test we can diagnose the carriers of each of these three genotypes. It would then be possible to go through the population of 100 persons and record what the genotype of each person is for this particular feature.

A population of 100 persons has a total of 200 genes at this one spot on the one chromosome which we are considering, because each person carries two, a pair, one on each of one pair of chromosomes. Let us say that the results of our study of the 100 persons shows the following: 81 persons are $I^B I^B$, and only one person is $I^A I^A$. It is obvious that in the gene pool in which these people share, the gene for the A mucopolysaccharide is rarer than its alternative, I^B. We may specify the exact frequency of the I^A gene in the gene pool of the population of adults now present on the island. One hundred people are carrying 200 genes at this locus and we may ask, then, what is the frequency of the I^A gene among these 200? The single $I^A I^A$ person carries two such genes, so that there are two I^A genes from this source. Each $I^A I^B$ person contributes only one I^A gene. As there are 18 such persons, there will be 18 I^A genes from this source. The total number of I^A genes will be $2 + 18 = 20$. Thus there will be 20 I^A genes out of a possible 200. The gene frequency of I^A in the island gene pool is 10 percent. The remainder, 90 percent, are I^B genes.

Now, with this information about the young adult population on the island, we can predict the blood groups found among the people of the next generation. The best way to visualize this is to make a model of the gene pool. Take 90 red poker chips and 10 white poker chips and mix them up in a bowl. This models the gene pool of the population as regards the gene dealing with blood types. The white chips represent the 10 percent I^A genes and the red chips represent the remaining I^B genes. Now we can simulate the reproductive act by drawing out two chips from this bowl. These represent the egg and sperm. The drawing and combination should be performed blindly, wholly at random, like the reproductive process. Obviously, the pair will be either both red ($I^B I^B$), both white ($I^A I^A$), or one of each ($I^A I^B$).

After trying this a few times, it is obvious that the chance of getting the genotype which would result in a child with an A blood group ($I^A I^A$) is much lower than that of either of the other two. The chance of getting such a result depends strictly on how frequent the white chips are in the bowl. Actually, it is easy to calculate that on the average only one in a hundred such draws will result in an $I^A I^A$ individual. By making a large series of drawings the genes are represented in certain frequencies from pools in which a prediction may be made as to the numbers of A, B, and AB blood groups that will appear in the population in the next generation. This relationship between the frequency of a gene in the gene pool and the frequency of the genetic types of individuals which are formed at reproduction is one of the automatic consequences of the mechanism of heredity. It forms one of the fundamental theorems of population genetics and applies to all genes.[1]

The study of the genetics of human populations has depended to a very great extent on our ability to recognize and identify individual genes and to measure their individual frequencies. As was previously emphasized, many human attributes, including extremely important ones like mental capacities, are affected by many individual genes. Each of these may have such a small effect alone that it is not possible to identify the gene individually as such without elaborate experimental work, the likes of which is obviously both undesirable and impossible with the human species.

Some years ago, human population genetics was able to use for gene-frequency studies only certain rather rare genes such as that for albinism. Not only are such genes very infrequent in most populations but most are recessive, so that the carriers cannot ordinarily be recognized; externally they have perfectly normal pigmentation. Thus, if our hypothetical island population had a 10 percent frequency of the albino gene, only one person in 100 would be an albino. Among the remaining 99, there would be no way to distinguish the 18 carriers from the 81 other normally pigmented persons. Biochemical genetics, however, has come to the rescue. In the blood alone, nearly 50 genetic differences can be specified by simple chemical examinations. In many cases, like the example given, carriers can be recognized by simple chemical examinations. Unlike some superficial characters like hair color, the effects of the genes cannot be changed by the whim of the person who has them. Accordingly, the study of gene frequencies in various human gene pools now rests on a large body of factual data. Even though we cannot safely use characters with a complex heredity for this purpose, we are now able to speak with much greater authority about human gene pools than when we were confined to rare recessives like albinism.

The genetic nature of populations, then, is best described in terms of the frequencies of particular genes, taken one by one, in its gene pool. Both the gene frequency and the individual A blood group genotype frequency that results from it (10 percent and 1 percent, respectively, in our example) will remain the same in the population from generation to generation as long as the following conditions are fulfilled. First, marriage must be at random within the population, that is to say that any one man on the island must choose his wife from the whole population, not just some exclusive division of it. For instance, if persons with A blood group married only others like themselves, this would tend to divide the gene pool into two gene pools. Second, the capacity to reproduce must be the same for persons of all three genotypes. If, for instance, an $I^B I^B$ mother has on the average more children than the other two types of mothers, the gene frequency of the I^A gene would be reduced from one generation to the next. There are other forces as well that operate to change gene frequencies; these will be discussed in the next chapter.

The importance of processes which reduce, generation by generation, the frequency of a gene such as the one for A blood group or albinism is obvious. If these forces continued long enough, these rare genes might be eliminated from the population entirely; conversely, the B blood group or the gene for normal pigmentation would be the alternates remaining. Indeed, in isolated gene pools, some genes which the ancestral group had are "bred out" by marriage patterns or selection. Other perhaps new and different genes are "bred in" to the group. Despite genetic kinship between all men, the continual past subdivision of the human gene pool has promoted the accumulation of differences.

Another way of expressing the above is to say that evolution, descent with change, has occurred. The unit process of evolution is change in gene frequencies in populations, but unless some force favors one genotype over an alternate one, there will be no change at all.

Subdivisions of the gene pool

Let us return to consideration of the hypothetical island population, diagrammed in Fig. 19. This population was derived from a single founding family which originally landed on the island. Such a situation would require marriages between brother and sister in the earliest stages of the development of the population, but after a few generations a more usual pattern of marriage between less closely related persons would be likely to follow. Nevertheless, the brief period during which marriage between very close relatives had of necessity to occur is of extreme importance in understanding the genetic nature of the descendant population. Although perhaps not as extreme or diagrammatic as this example, it is likely that many different human populations in past centuries have repeatedly passed through narrow bottlenecks.

Marriage between close relatives is called inbreeding. The degree of inbreeding is measured by the closeness of the relationship between the two marriage partners. The "closest" inbreeding possible in human populations is represented by marriage between parent-child or brother-sister. Following this come marriages such as uncle-niece or marriage between first cousins, second cousins, and so on. If, in a population, a large proportion of the marriages tend to be between relatively closely related persons, even if the relationship is more distant than cousins, this population may be described as relatively inbred.

Isolation of an area by geographical factors, as islands or remote mountain villages are isolated, usually has meant that the human migrants reaching these places have arrived in a small band initially and have remained thereafter in a small population. Such populations are very frequently closely inbred ones, by virtue of the small beginning bottleneck and the continued relatively small size.

Contrary to popular notion, inbreeding does not automatically have bad consequences. Nevertheless, the more closely related two persons are, the more likely each of them is to carry some of the same recessive genes. Marriage between two such persons results, as we have seen, in a high probability of producing a child which is homozygous for one of these genes (see Fig. 5). As many recessive genes in man turn out to be somewhat detrimental in double dose, marriage between two such persons increases the chance that a defective child may be produced. It is interesting to speculate that the widespread taboo on marriages of close relatives in human societies may have originated because observation showed that such marriages carried with them the likelihood of such harmful results. On the other hand, when good luck prevails, when such "bad" genes are either not present in one partner or do not come together, the individual born of a marriage of close relatives has no intrinsic undesirable characteristics arising out of the fact that his parents were related. In and by itself, inbreeding is not bad, although the genetic situation frequently suggests that it would be wise to avoid close inbreeding.

Our island population therefore might be expected to show a somewhat elevated frequency of genetic defects. Albinism serves as a suitable example. This population, furthermore, at the stage reached in Fig. 19b, would not by any means be without genetic variability just because all members of the population are descended from a very few ancestors. New mutations can have occurred since the time of colonization but, much more importantly, the genes existing in the two original founding parents would have been recombined, by the chance chromosomal processes of sexual reproduction, into many unique descendant combinations, in our example, 100 new, different ones (persons) four generations later. Despite mutation and recombination, however, such a population would be likely to show relatively low genetic variability, principally because of its inbred nature. For this effect to be striking, however, inbreeding in small populations would have to continue for something like 30 or 60 generations.

Figures 19c and 19d represent hypothetical future changes in the island population which would continue the tradition for occasional migration followed by inbreeding and isolation. In 19c, the village has grown larger; there have still been no new migrations to the island, but one family has migrated from the west village across the mountains and settled on the east shore.

Whereas the village of 100 persons shown in Fig. 19b represented an integrated intermarrying community, that is, a true single gene pool, the situation has become somewhat different by the time the village has grown to the stage we find in Fig. 19c. The spreading out of the village has resulted in partially isolated "north-village" and "south-village" sections. Human associations being what they are, it is obvious that a marriage is more likely between persons coming from the same part of the village. A human community of any size is always affected by this geographical rule; the majority of marriages even under modern urban conditions are between persons who live close to one another in a geographical sense. The "north-village" and "south-village" separation would have the effect of restricting gene flow through the gene pool. If this tendency continued, the original single gene pool would become divided into two partially connected gene pools.

Obviously, the single family that migrated across the mountains has had an even greater effect in subdividing the island gene pool; Fig. 19d shows a possible later stage. A second village has grown up on the east shore, repeating to some degree the history of the first village, even to forming two sections, one north and one south of the bay. The gene pool on the island now has two major subdivisions with additional minor subdivisions. In discussing gene-pool subdivision, we have deliberately emphasized conditions favoring such division. Separation would be enhanced by the absence of islandwide festivals, by taboos on marriage with any but a close neighbor, and by the custom of living a sedentary, nonexploratory existence. As diagrammed, the factors involved would promote a pattern of inbreeding in small populations, a process which would have a divisive effect on the gene pool of the island population, tending to cut it up into isolates. This would be conducive to genetic divergence.

Contrasted to the extreme just outlined, consider the situation resulting from human occupation of the same island under conditions and tendencies different from the above. Let us assume (Fig. 20) that the colonization was originally made by a small band of three families. Intermarriage between families would prevent the situation of close inbreeding found in the other example. The single gene pool found after four generations (Fig. 20b) would be no larger than the one in the other example, but the amount of variability within the population would be greater because the founders were not so few in number and not so inbred. At the stage of the formation of a second village on the island (Figs. 20c and 20d) migration in this case again involves a number of families, so that this new village is started with a relatively large sample of genes from the original village. No tendency is encountered which strongly promotes marriage within sections of the villages. Communication between the villages is kept open by migration back and forth. In addition, occasional migrant families continue to arrive on the island and are integrated into the breeding structure of the community.

The example just given would contrast with the former in that the island population in this case would represent a single undivided gene pool. Occasional flow of genes in from the outside would tend to keep the variability high. The system could be described as one of moderate outbreeding, the tendency for marriages to occur between relatively unrelated persons. Such a designation, it should always be remembered, is a relative matter. The term outbreeding or outcrossing can be used to refer to marriages between two persons of slightly different ancestry within the same gene pool. A slightly wider outcross might be between persons coming from two different subdivisions of a barely divided gene pool, such as the "north village" or "south village" in the earlier example. An even wider outcross would be represented by marriage between individuals coming from different islands.

Just as the closest type of inbreeding is represented by mating within the immediate family, so the widest possible outbreeding would be between two individuals drawn from groups of the

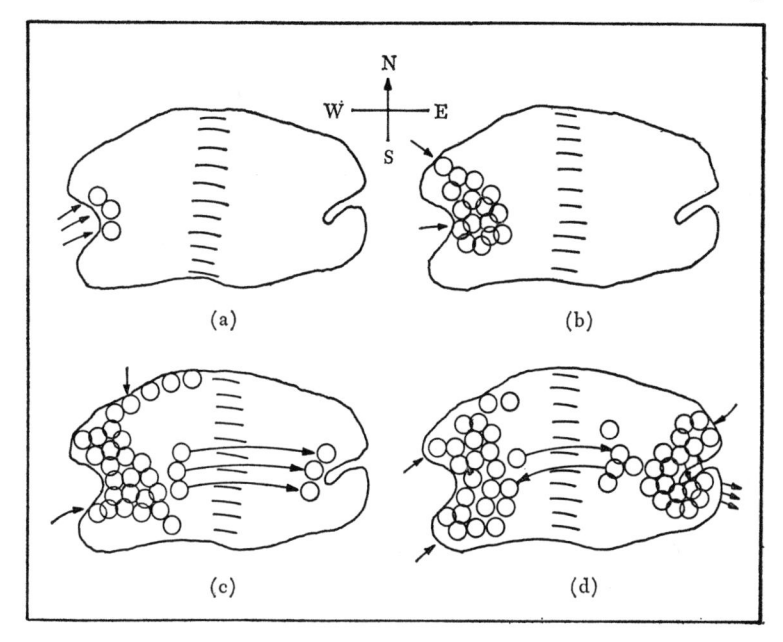

Fig. 20. Population founding under conditions where the gene pool remains single with moderate outbreeding

(a) Island colonized by three couples. There will be an avoidance of close inbreeding because of the opportunities for marriage between families. (b) Small population derived from (a) about four generations later. Two new migrant families have arrived and have been integrated into the community which forms a single gene pool with considerably more genetic variability than was present in the population diagrammed in Fig. 19b. (c) Same island a few generations later. The west village is larger, is essentially undivided, and has received more migrant families. Three families have migrated over the mountain range and settled on the east shore. (d) Island now has two villages but, as arrows indicate, continuous migrations and integrations occur. The east and west villages, although partially isolated by distance, really form a single gene pool, as marriage frequently occurs within and between villages. Genetic variability remains high throughout the island because of genetic recombination.

human species which have been widely separated in space and time for very long periods, such as a South American Indian and an aborigine from southern Australia. In most cases, however, inbreeding and outbreeding refer to some intermediate condition; these intermediate cases have had by far the greatest effect in conditioning the genetic structure of human populations.

As we shall see in later discussions, much of the history of the genes of mankind on this planet can be understood in terms of cycles of inbreeding and outbreeding. Inbreeding tends to make the gene pool concerned relatively easy to specify and to study, whereas outbreeding tends to promote the combination and recombination of what might once have been quite separate gene pools. The complexity of the situation makes it necessary, before going further, to examine the origin of the human species and the forces which brought this about, and then to try to trace the subsequent history of human gene pools up to the present time.

Summary

The most important level of genetic organization above that of the individual is the reproductive community that we call the population. Thus, the individual does not exist alone; in a very real biological sense the genetic properties of the population to which he belongs are those of a mathematical pool. Each reproductive set draws a combination of genes from the pool and incarnates this combination as one individual. These new individuals become, in turn, members of the population of the next generation. In this manner the gene pool is handed on from generation to generation. An island population with no barriers to crossing among its members and no immigrants would be a diagrammatic example of a single, undivided gene pool. In order to study the behavior of genes in the pool, each gene must be identified individually. In actual studies, characters having a simple hereditary basis must be used; biochemical characters have been strongly emphasized in recent years. The basic datum is the frequency of particular genes. If the frequency is known, precise predictions about the number of people showing the effects of the gene, or carrying it, can be made.

The mechanisms of Mendelian heredity are very conservative and tend to keep gene frequencies the same from generation to generation. This rule holds, however, only if persons carrying different genotypes have, on the average, the same number of children. If this is so, then the gene pool of the generation represented by the children will have the same composition as that of the previous one. If carriers of a certain genotype consistently outbreed other genotypes, that is, are favored by selection, this will result in a generation by generation change in the frequency of a gene. The eventual result will be either virtual elimination of the gene or the opposite, that is, its fixation at 100 percent in the gene pool. Whenever a population grows large, what was formerly one gene pool tends to become subdivided into a number of smaller, partially connected ones. If the isolation is great and the individual segments of the gene pools small, the genetic situation known as inbreeding or mating between relatively closely related individuals occurs within these segments. Conversely, crossing between individuals derived from two relatively isolated gene pools may be referred to as outbreeding. All degrees of both conditions occur and both have been of utmost importance in the past history of the genetic material in human gene pools.

Chapter 7

ORIGIN OF THE HUMAN SPECIES

WHERE and when did man evolve? What were the sizes and the distribution of prehuman and early human populations? Can we explain the present physical and cultural diversity of human groups by recourse to prehistory? How many of these differences between us are due to gene differences between the gene pools of the present subdivisions of men? Scientific answers to most of these questions have resulted from the quiet labors of thousands of biologists over the last hundred years.

When we examine a present-day species there are two main questions that we ask about it. The first question deals with the course of its past history. We want to know what its many ancestors looked like, what their behavior was like, and what their habits were. We must reconstruct, descriptively, the flow of millions of years of history; we want to know just what the pathways of descent have been. Second, we may ask what the forces were which guided the changes in the gene pools of the past along certain lines. Why were some genes preserved and others not? These questions are embodied in two sciences: paleontology, which digs up remnants and pieces together the biological past, and population genetics, which seeks causes for permanent change in the composition of gene pools.

The ancestors of man

The outlines of the prehistory of the human species are now at least dimly known from sparse but very meaningful fossil remains. Those who are tempted to scoff at the incompleteness of the record should be reminded that absolutely everything that is known comes from remains that were preserved by sheer lucky chance in the first place. Every link and branch will be missing, furthermore, until someone finds a site, gathers the shreds of evidence, and starts the process of reconstruction of an ancient mode of life by inference from these shreds. The most important evidence dealing with a form like man comes from bones or fragments of bones. Comparative anatomy, especially as it applies to the skeleton, is an ancient, stable, and sound branch of biology. From the facts discovered by anatomists we know that the bones of an animal are meaningful down to the finest detail. Because muscles attach to bones, much can be inferred about the appearance of an animal from its bones, but even beyond that, certain parts, such as the teeth, not only are a biological "book" on the food habits of their possessor, but have a uniqueness which is unmistakable. An ape tooth is as great a misfit in a human jaw as a square peg is in a round hole.

There is no longer any doubt that the continent of Africa is the place where most of the key evolutionary events in the origin of man occurred. It is interesting that even before the remarkable new fossil finds in Africa were made the biological relationships of the human species made it possible for Darwin to suggest that man must have originated on the African continent. He based his suppositions on the fact that the two closest relatives of the human species in the animal kingdom, the gorilla and the chimpanzee, appear to have originated in Africa and have remained there until the present day as wild animals. Gorilla and chimpanzee as well as their two somewhat more specialized relatives from the Indonesian islands, the orangutan and gibbon, are apes and should not be confused with monkeys. Monkeys from both the Eastern and the Western hemispheres have a body structure which indicates that their relationship to man is far more distant than that of the four types of "great ape." The most conspicuous manlike feature of the apes is the fact that they lack tails, but there are many other important features, including corresponding details of skeleton and the general strong development of the brain. No amount of sentimentalizing or anthropomorphism, however, can alter the fact that the highly personable chimpanzee is in every scientific sense nonhuman. Here again lies the paradox of relationship. Although apes are our closest relatives in the animal kingdom, this relationship is still quite remote.

How far must we go back in biological history to be able to say that we share a common ancestor with our closest animal relatives? Recent fossil discoveries now permit us to give quite a clear answer. The human line of descent has been separate from that of the great apes for about 25 million years. On the face of it this may sound like a very long time and indeed it is. The fossil record of life, however, can be read from favorable rocks over quite vast periods of time; paleontologists deal quite routinely with fossils many of which are old, some more than 500 million years. Viewed comparatively, then, 25 million years is a short time ago. Comparative anatomical studies establish man as belonging to the Mammalia, the great class of backboned animals that arose between 70 and 100 million years ago. This whole group was much more successful than the reptiles which preceded it, largely because of improved brains and sense organs and the high-temperature chemical systems that we describe as "warm-bloodedness."

One particular line of descent of mammals showed from the

very earliest a tendency towards especially great development of the brain and its communication system, the sense organs. The modern order of mammals that followed this line is called the Primates; it includes monkeys, apes, and man as well as odd forms which arose from the primate family tree quite early in its history—the lemurs, tarsiers, and lorises.

The Primates are newcomers and all indications are that man as a species is of extraordinarily recent origin. To return to the figure of 25 million years mentioned above, this is the approximate age of an exceptionally important group of fossils which has been found in recent years in Kenya in East Africa. Of particular interest is a form which has been called *Proconsul;* it is the fossil animal that most closely relates modern man to the modern great apes. *Proconsul* is a fascinating find because it is neither modern ape nor modern man, but it has some features that are found separately in both of these present-day forms. We cannot say that *Proconsul* was strictly an ape because in many ways it was quite unlike the modern chimpanzee or gorilla. At the same time, *Proconsul* was more like man than the modern apes, but this degree of resemblance does not justify calling *Proconsul* "manlike."

If the above seems confusing, it is largely because of our narrow perspective. We tend to think in terms only of "men" or "apes" as we know them today. We, as humans, are not descended from apes any more than apes, as we know them today, are descended from us. The only way to escape the confusion is to continually remind ourselves that ancestral forms, especially those that appear to be common to two modern descended groups, were always precise, adapted, living species in their own right. Usually, they are quite different from anything existing today.

Abundant remains of *Proconsul* have been found and there were apparently a number of sizes of them, ranging from one the size of a large monkey to one resembling the gorilla in size. The skull gives the general impression of an ape, but is nonapelike because it has smooth brows and lacks the shelflike reinforcement of the lower jaw that is found in modern apes. The limbs are such that *Proconsul* must have been terrestrial in habit like both man and apes, suggesting that the tree-swinging gibbons separated from this line of descent much earlier. *Proconsul's* gait was probably apelike; it must have proceeded on all fours but sometimes must have stood erect. Certain features of the arm foreshadow human characteristics.

All things considered, a conservative judgment of *Proconsul* places him definitely on the ape branch, rather than just at the point where ape and human lines diverge. (See Fig. 21.) Yet of all fossil remains found so far, this one links us most closely to other living species. Nevertheless, from this time on, our line of development has been clearly separate from that of the apes.

The especially exciting newer discoveries of primate fossils on the African continent, however, come from deposits which are very much younger, in fact, all are somewhat less than two million years old. Very little is known about the line leading towards man between this more recent date and the time of separation from the great ape line. Inference from family trees of other living things, however, makes it very likely that the line of descent was an indirect one with a number of branches coming off and subsequently dying out, as suggested in Fig. 21. There is no reason to believe that during this time there was a single-line tendency towards the present human form.

At the present time, only one set of fossils can be placed into this long gap; these are the ones known as *Oreopithecus,* a curious primate of about 10 million years ago. These fossils come from caves in central Italy and consist mostly of jaw and skull fragments, so that whether *Oreopithecus* walked upright is not known. Characteristics of face, teeth, and skull definitely exclude this animal both from the monkeys and the apes, but the resemblance to humans is only vague and general. Many workers have pointed out that such primitiveness is just what might be expected at this particular stage in history, yet most feel that it is safer to accord *Oreopithecus* a position well off the more direct line which must have been leading in a human direction at that time.

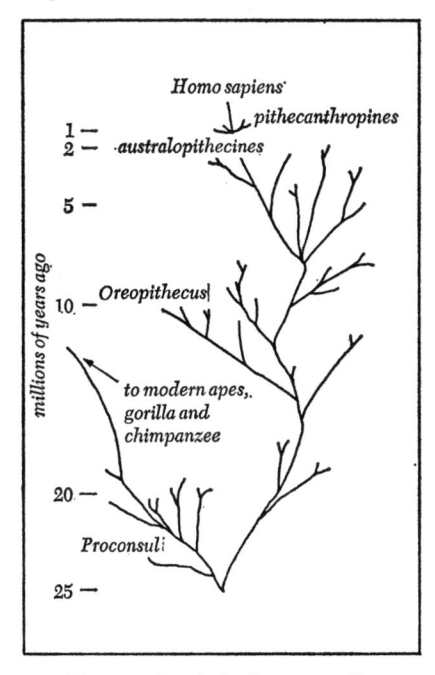

Fig. 21. Time scale of the last 25 million years of earth history, together with an interpretative diagram of the evolution of apelike and manlike forms

As indicated in the text, the many fine branches are hypothetical; they are intended to suggest the inescapable conclusion that the fossils which have been found represent only a few of the many lines that did exist.

No such uncertainty, however, surrounds those forms which have been called the australopithecines, a very striking group of "near-men." Rich fossil remains of these forms are known from South Africa, and more recently they have been found farther north in East Africa. In stature, most of them were quite small, but unquestionably they were ground-dwelling; their remains are found in places which indicate that they were living in open grassland areas. Of special interest, however, is the fact that their pelvic structure is distinctly of the human, not ape, type, so that it is clear that they stood quite erect. On the other hand, their skulls and the brains were very small when judged by modern human standards; the essential characteristics of the human brain had not yet been evolved. The tendency towards the human, however, is strikingly reflected in the structure of the teeth; these show detailed resemblances to humans rather than apes. The biggest difference is that in some cases the jaws are massive and the teeth very large. As a final note of importance, the australopithecines show a forehead which is smooth above the eyes, without heavy brow ridges, a feature which should be remembered as the story of the Ice Age men unfolds.

The most sensational recent finds of australopithecine fossils have been made at Olduvai Gorge in Tanganyika.[1] These earliest "near-men" come from deposits which are generally acknowledged to have been laid down about 1,750,000 years ago and the remains, taken from this bed, are accordingly judged to be of this age. This would make them older than the beginning of the Pleistocene Ice Age, which is generally dated at approximately one million years ago. Two major fossil finds have been made at this site. The better preserved of the two is the form which was named *Zinjanthropus*. This was an australopithecine which is remarkable for the number of features of the skull which bear a strong resemblance to that of modern man. Although the height of the skull is low and the brain size characteristically small like that of the South African australopithecines, the facial architecture is distinctive and foreshadows the human condition. In other ways, however, *Zinjanthropus* shows signs of being specialized, like the later australopithecines. That this form is off the direct line of human descent is also indicated by the details of the second major fossil type from the early bed of Olduvai Gorge, this was part of the skull of a twelve-year-old boy which was found in 1961. This form definitely lacks the special characters and, although it is from older deposits, had a larger brain capacity than *Zinjanthropus* and the later australopithecines.

Most striking of all is the definite association of both of these forms with primitive tools, some of which were fashioned from bone, whereas others were crude choppers made from hand-sized pebbles with one face chipped off. These are the so-called pebble tools of the Oldowan culture, the oldest known of Stone Age implements. Along with the tools are remains of many small birds, rats, lizards, and fish, and only a few larger mammals, such as immature pigs and antelopes.

One cannot escape the conclusion that despite the small brains possessed by the australopithecines we are seeing for the first time the development of a culture. In this technical sense, culture may be defined as a design for living which is passed down from generation to generation. The regular use of tools implies that the groups concerned had this capacity, and that they used tools to a set and regular pattern rather than haphazardly and sporadically. Another implication also follows; this is that some sort of verbal communication would be expected to accompany such a culture. The palate structure of *Zinjanthropus* as well as his brain conformation were certainly capable of supporting speech, although there is no crucial evidence on this point.

When does a "near-man" become a man? No one can make any sensible rule to follow. When talking or writing about these fossils it is necessary to use various noncommittal terms, like "early forms," "fossils," and so on. "Ape-man," "man-ape," or other such designations should be avoided because of their rather oversimplified connotations. When most of us speak of "man" or "humans" we think in terms of representatives of living populations that we see here on earth today. Our type of man is a far cry from the australopithecines, so that when we emphasize the humanlike qualities of the latter we must not be carried away. The emergence of man as we know him today came gradually, and these early stages now under discussion were still quite removed from what we recognize today as characteristic of *Homo sapiens*. However, their closeness to man is emphasized by the fact that they are apparently separated from the apes by about 23 million years of separate evolution.

The first detailed descriptions and general knowledge of the australopithecines came from the study of extraordinarily rich and abundant fossil remains which have been found in South Africa.[2] Two major forms have been described, *Australopithecus* and *Paranthropus*. Both appear to be in deposits which are much more recent than those of the Tanganyika australopithecines. In fact, both of them may have survived from about the beginning of the Ice Age (one million years ago) to the middle of the Ice Age (500,000 years ago). The dates, however, are somewhat uncertain. A curious fact, mentioned previously, stands out: *Australopithecus* and *Paranthropus* do not represent stages more like man than, for instance, *Zinjanthropus*, despite the fact that they are younger. Close study leads one to the conclusion that we are not seeing in these forms the direct ancestors of modern man. Both of them, for instance, have skeletal and tooth structures which show signs of being specialized in a way that we, today, are not. At most, only a few pebble tools are associated with them. Trends towards specialization are rarely reversed in evolution, so that the most commonly drawn conclusion is that in these, at least, we have found not a direct ancestor but a side branch which was not progressing directly towards man.

The upper part of Fig. 21 gives the writer's view of the way the facts add up, with the direct line of human descent passing somewhere closer to *Zinjanthropus* than to the later australopithecines. The great improbability of striking a fossil which is just on the crucial line of descent has been mentioned before (Fig. 21); furthermore, it suggests that myriads of side branches have been continually formed and lost and that we have been able to find only a few points on the family tree. In paleontology, like any other science, there is no information at all until someone actually digs something up and describes it.

Back of the so-called "recent epoch," which comprises approximately the last 10,000 years of world history, lies the Ice Age or Pleistocene epoch (see Fig. 22). This began about a million years ago and during it a series of four advances and four retreats of great ice sheets took place (shaded areas in Fig. 22). There is no good evidence that the australopithecines ever migrated out of Africa, but somewhere around a half a million years ago, in the middle Pleistocene, some primitive groups did spread from Africa into Asia. The remains of this group are best known from fossils which have been found in Java (*Pithecanthropus* or Java man) and on the Chinese mainland near Peking (Peking man). These fossils, for which the term pithecanthropine will be used, are very similar to each other but very different from both australopithecines and modern man. The most striking point is the development in them of heavy, bony brow ridges, sometimes of very large size. The skulls were massive and heavy, with a low and sloping forehead and protruded lower face. Brain size, while larger than the australopithecines, is nonetheless small. Some, at least the later ones (Trinil and Solo), used crude tools of the chopper type, not very advanced over those found with the autralopithecines. Peking "man," however, made use of fire.

Pithecanthropinelike forms were not confined to the Far East; a number of finds in Africa show affinity to them. Perhaps the most important of these is a find made in 1961 by Leakey in one of the more recent beds in Olduvai Gorge, dating from approximately 400,000 years ago, over a million years younger than the bed in which *Zinjanthropus* was found. This form had, unlike the australopithecines, enormous, heavy brow ridges, suggesting affinity to the pithecanthropines. Even more significant is the definite association of this skull with a particular type of

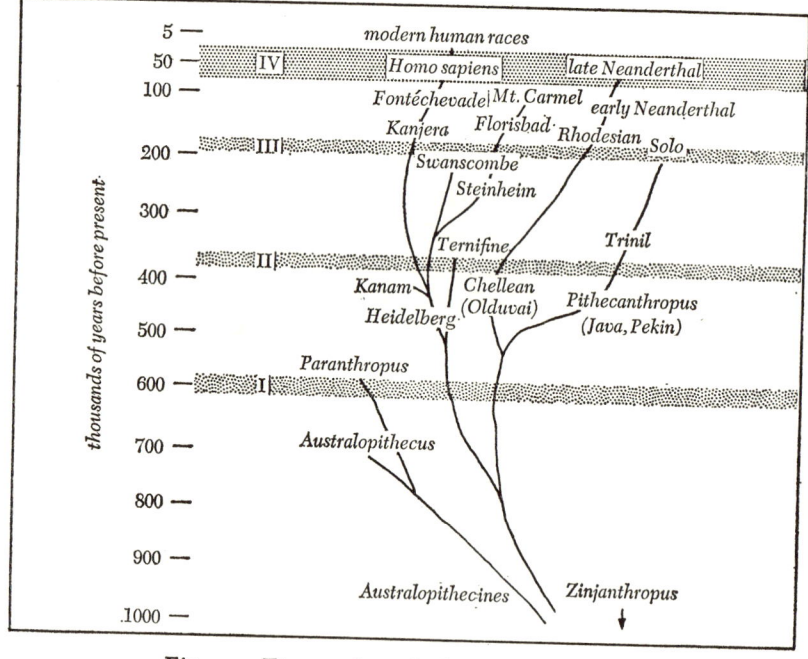

Fig. 22. Time scale of the last million years of earth history, the Pleistocene

The known manlike fossil forms are arranged in an interpretative diagram. The four advances of the glacial ice are indicated by the dotted bands. The extraordinary recency of modern man (*Homo sapiens*) is apparent.

hand ax which has been found in later Pleistocene deposits all over Africa and even into Europe. This hand ax, called Chellean (Chelles-Acheul culture) is a definite advance over the earlier pebble tools and suggests that the maker had progressed in inventiveness. It now seems clear that the earliest makers of these hand axes were heavy-browed pithecanthropine types.

Now let us come to the most difficult point. As we will see, brow-ridged fossils dominate the scene from this point on in the story until extremely recently, a matter of a mere 35,000 years ago. Yet today's type of man, whether he be Bushman, Eskimo, or Caucasian, definitely does not have these brow ridges. The writer agrees with those who consider that all of the very heavy-browed types are off the main track leading to modern man. This includes not only the lineage in the Far East, that is, *Pithecanthropus*-Trinil-Solo, but also those very recent, heavy-browed, rather specialized, and uninventive inhabitants of Africa, Europe, and western Asia, namely, Rhodesian and Neanderthal "men" (see Fig. 22).

Neanderthal, the "cave man" of popular legend, appears to be the culmination of this line of descent, an extraordinary blind alley of forms, remnants of which have been found in gratifying abundance in caves all over Europe (except Britain and the northern countries), North Africa, and western Asia. Rhodesian man, a very heavy brow-ridged form from Broken Hill, Northern Rhodesia, and Saldanha Bay, South Africa, was an approximate contemporary of Solo man of the Far East. He appears to be in the same line of descent.

Neanderthal fossils are extraordinarily recent. They first appear just before the last ice sheet, and this form of life became extinct only about 50,000 years ago. The earliest ones had big brows and a very large face. The sides of the head were relatively low, as compared with our species. The face projected forward at the mouth, and the jaw, correspondingly, receded. In denying that they were our direct ancestors, one should not underestimate the success and prevalence of both the Neanderthals and their other heavy-browed relatives. They were efficient hunters of the larger Ice Age mammals, using tools of a characteristic sort; they employed fire and, at least in some instances, buried their dead.

Before the Neanderthals died out during the advance of the last ice sheet, a change in structure ensued. The body of the later Neanderthal became more massive and heavy, the head became even lower and more bulging and the dental arches were heavier. These later Neanderthals were barrel-chested and bull-necked and there is some indication of bowed limbs. In all these features they are unlike modern man; thus we see again the extraordinary evolutionary phenomenon of a very recent and distinctly manlike form progressing away from the condition of modern man during the same time that modern man was arising from other ancestors.

The blind alley, one of the most striking attributes of the evolutionary process in countless others forms of life, clearly lies here before us in this most striking and pertinent case. It is hard to escape the conclusion that all of the big-browed African, European, and Far Eastern forms are off the line that concerns us most.

The emergence of Homo sapiens

How clear is the existence of a second, major, nonpithecanthropine line leading to us, with our high-domed, smooth-browed heads? A number of African Middle Eastern, and European fossils seem to fit into such a lineage but the story is less clear, unfortunately, than it is for the big-browed line. Of nine fossil forms which might be placed in this line prior to the appearance of our species, *Homo sapiens*, four are African, four are European, and one (Mount Carmel) is from Palestine (Fig. 22). The three oldest, Heidelberg (Germany), Kanam (East Africa), and Ternafine (Algeria) are represented principally by jaws, so that the crucial condition of the brow ridges and forehead is unknown.

Both Heidelberg and Kanam, however, are definitely not of the pithecanthropine type. They have smaller teeth and the latter has, most interestingly, a prominent chin. This latter is a good characteristic feature of *Homo sapiens* and is unknown among any of the brow-ridge forms.

The Ternafine jaw, however, has attributes that relate it to the pithecanthropines, yet the definitive parts that would affirm this decision have not been found.

Two most important brain cases are known from deposits of the second interglacial period, Swanscombe, England, and Steinheim, Germany. Steinheim has moderate brow ridges which are separated over the nose, unlike Chellean (Olduvai) or Neanderthal. In the case of Swanscombe, the crucial frontal bones are missing so that the brow condition cannot be determined. Neither of these fossils, furthermore, has associated jaws which would enable them to be interpreted in terms of the three jaws mentioned previously. Their remarkable features, however, are connected with the shape of the skull. Both show a tendency towards a high forehead and vertical sides, features that are definitely unlike Neanderthal, Rhodesian, or pithecanthropine. Swanscombe is associated with late-stage hand axes and there is evidence of the use of fire.

Coming closer to the present, two fragmentary skulls, one found at Kanjera in East Africa and one at Fontéchevade in France, appear to combine third interglacial period antiquity with almost entirely modern human skull structures. Neither of these skulls gives any evidence of brow ridges and in both the dome of the skull was at least as high as is found in Swanscombe and Steinheim. Fontéchevade is particularly important because it shows that men very similar to ourselves existed simultaneously with the Neanderthals.

Two other sets of skulls should be mentioned, both are quite recent and apparently their owners also coexisted with the Neanderthals; these are represented by the quite well preserved Florisbad skull from South Africa and the extraordinary series of remains found in caves on Mount Carmel in Palestine. Both of these combine the features of moderately large but somewhat separate ridges over both eyes with a relatively high dome to the forehead and sides of the skull. These four are certainly by far the closest to our species of any of the other remains which have been mentioned. The Mount Carmel finds are especially interesting because of the variation among the individuals found in one place in the cave. This variation has been interpreted in various ways: some feel that there is evidence of hybridization between an unknown prehuman stock and Neanderthal men. Others, like the present writer, take the more conservative view that the Mount Carmel forms were a variable offshoot from the main line of human descent which is represented by Fontéchevade and Kanjera. In any event, there is room at this point for disagreement only over the interpretation of details. Refinements of our knowledge will continue to be made as new fossils are found and the newer methods of dating are applied.

The next chapter of the story begins a mere 35,000 years ago. This is the appearance of abundant fossil remains of modern men of a type that is wholly similar to *Homo sapiens* as he exists today. His remains are unmistakable. Here is the high dome of the skull, with its light, almost delicate, brain case, the high forehead, the prominent chin, and the characteristic dental arch. Our kind of man now appears in a manner that can only be described as "suddenly"; in countless caves his remains lie just above those of the brutish Neanderthals in the Middle East and Europe. Associated with him we now find the remains of imaginative and rapidly advancing culture. Engraving, carving, and painting appear, as well as personal adornments of various kinds. Quickly, in but a moment compared with the slow plodding of the primitives over hundreds of thousands of years, we find the new

Stone Age yielding to Bronze, Bronze to Iron, and, indeed, the Iron Age yielding to Atomic Age. The culture of *Homo sapiens* exploded on the earth, starting a mere thousand generations or so ago. It began with small bands of ancestors who expanded into the billions we have today.

Consider the briefness of the time involved. It is no trouble for us to conceive of the time passed since the Christian era: 2,000 years. Four thousand years further back brings us to Ur and the early civilizations of the Middle East. Another 4,000 years back and we reach the round number of 10,000. To reach back four times as far, to 40,000 years ago, seems not impossible to visualize. Biologically speaking it is but a moment, when we compare it with the time passed, nearly 40 times as long, since the first australopithecines and their pebble tools. The three billion individuals that now comprise the human species have a very close bond of genetic relationship that they surely would not have had if the earlier geographical movements had left forms existing to the present day. They did not; Java "man," the Neanderthals, Rhodesian "man," Solo "men," and even the Mount Carmel types did not leave descendants to coexist with us. You who read this are united to the rest of mankind by a close bond of common descent.

Summary

The human species evolved in Africa. Its line of descent separated from that of the great apes about 25 million years ago. Ancestral populations between one and two million years ago consisted of ground-dwelling, upright, small-bodied, and small-brained grassland forms which used crude pebble tools. Manlike forms arising from such a stock first spread out of the African continent about 500,000 years ago, in the middle Pleistocene. These forms had heavy brow ridges and heavy skulls with brains inferior to those which characterize the modern human species. Such forms were successful and widespread; they persisted in eastern Asia for several hundred thousand years but the evidence indicates that they left no modern descendants.

A second branch of the brow-ridged group, having somewhat similar characteristics, remained in Africa and produced descendants who spread into adjacent areas of Europe and Asia. No direct descendants of these forms, including the aberrant and very recent Neanderthal "man," survive to the present day. All modern men, of whatever geographical origin, are of the species *Homo sapiens* which appeared as a separate development, probably in the middle Pleistocene about 400,000 years ago, and was completed approximately 40,000 years ago. Early fossil forms apparently leading towards man have been found about equally in Europe and Africa and are characterized by a tendency towards lighter, more delicate skulls which have high, rounded domes and at most only moderate brow ridges. The superior brain capacity of our modern species is immediately apparent in deposits 40,000 years old or less. *Homo sapiens* is easily recognizable by the evidence of rapid cultural advances, art, inventiveness, personal adornment, complex and intelligent food-gathering, hunting methods, and social organization. The full capacity of the human brain evolved before the final spread of man and the formation of the modern geographical races. Two things are remarkable about the evolution of man during the million years of the Ice Age: it involved primarily one organ, the brain, and the final perfection of the brain was recent and rapid.

Chapter 8

EVOLUTIONARY FORCES AS APPLIED TO MAN

WHEN one contemplates the emergence of the human species over the last million years or so of earth history, two things stand out. First, almost all the key changes since the australopithecine era have been in a single organ, the brain. Before the australopithecine discoveries, it was a matter for speculation whether upright posture and use of tools were features which followed the evolutionary development of the brain or whether they preceded it and essentially opened the way for its final evolution. We now have clear evidence that the latter is true. The australopithecines, making simple bone and pebble tools, and walking fully upright, had extremely small cranial capacities. Their descendants of the middle Pleistocene, however, showed a big change in the size, complexity, and functional properties of the brain. This brings us to the second feature of human evolution that is especially interesting and has been recently clarified. The brain, as we know it in modern man, evolved very rapidly, its whole perfection being completed in a period of around 500,000 years. By most evolutionary standards, this is very fast.

Are there other instances of fast evolution of single organs in other evolutionary histories? There are; in fact, it is almost an evolutionary commonplace to observe a rapid change in evolutionary rates.[1] One of the misconceptions that modern study of genetic change has dispelled is the idea that evolution always proceeds exceedingly slowly and always at the same rate. Indeed, cases are known in which evolution has essentially ceased for even hundreds of millions of years. Contrariwise, bursts of evolutionary change in a relatively small number of generations frequently have occurred such that the end result may erroneously lead us to believe that long geological epochs were involved. Much is now known about the genetic and populational conditions surrounding these bursts of change.

Natural selection

Evolution has one principal guiding force, natural selection. To be passed on from generation to generation, of course, any change in body or brain has to have an hereditary basis, that is, it must be based on a genic change. When a favorable mutation does occur, furthermore, this change is likely to be recessive and to be found at first in only one cell of one individual. Furthermore, only one of the two gene loci in that individual is changed. In order to become established as the "norm" throughout the population, this changed gene has to be present in double dose in a majority of the individuals. This is a long way from a single locus in a single individual.

More is required than the process of gene mutation if evolution is to proceed; in fact, it is at this juncture that the process of selection may be seen to be important. The actual process of mutation is undirected towards the needs of the living being. What happens, however, if this new mutation does turn out to be one of those rare ones which, in double dose, is more beneficial than the original condition? Carriers of this new condition will, on the average, have perhaps a few more offspring than noncarriers. This means that in the gene pool represented by these offspring, the new gene will be slightly more frequent.

In short, natural selection multiplies the good genes just a little faster than their alternatives. This is just another way of saying that individuals of some genotypes leave more offspring, on the average, than others.

This way of expressing the meaning of natural selection, in terms of one genotype outbreeding another, may surprise some people, who may have thought that it is better described by "survival of the fittest" or some such favorite dramatic phrase. Now survival is, of course, essential, but it turns out to be more important to specify those, among the many survivors, who are most efficient in populating the next generation. These are the fittest. The fittest, in the evolutionary sense, is nothing more spectacular than the quiet, often unobtrusive fellow who, rather than spend his time struggling in combat, produces, feeds, and teaches a large family of children.

The biblical phrase "the meek shall inherit the earth" has a great ring of scientific truth about it. The biological future of any gene you have lies in the number of children to whom you transmit the gene and in the number of granchildren and great-grandchildren who possess it, in their turn. Any genetically determined trait, no matter what, which makes a man a better producer of a large and healthy family favors this particular line of descent just because this line makes a relatively large contribution to the composition of the gene pool of the next generation. Actually, the process can go on, and usually does, without any active struggle between the parties concerned.

Although this formulation may appeal to us ethically, we must be quick to point out that nature is not automatically ethical and good. Struggle and starvation do occur in nature as well as rigid pecking-orders and other phenomena that our ethical codes do not condone. We have often made the mistake of believing that we can find ethical codes ready-made for us by appealing to nonhuman nature. On the contrary, an ethical code of behavior is a product of the fully developed human brain; we ourselves, our thinkers and philosophers, have made it—the code is of human origin alone. Nature apart from us does not operate under any such code; we delude ourselves when we think we can be guided by what we fancy to be either the cooperations or the conflicts that go on among other forms of life.

How natural selection operates in natural populations may be visualized in the very clear example of change by selection of certain genes which has been observed in certain moths in England. Beginning about the time of the industrial revolution, tons of soot from the furnaces of the new factories and mills began to fall on the countryside around Birmingham, Manchester, and other cities in the midlands. Moths have existed in the forests in the area for millions of years and quite a number of them, especially night-flying ones, show a white-mottled, grayish pattern of coloration which renders them very inconspicuous on the grayish, lichen-covered tree trunks. In the case of some species, it has been possible to show that this gray coloration enables these moths to escape being eaten by birds. This has apparently been the outcome of an earlier selection; those grays which had the best protective coloration left the most offspring, gradually resulting in a perfection of protective resemblance.

When the blackening of the countryside began, the conditions which had existed for so long were suddenly changed. The gray lichens were killed by the soot in the polluted areas. In addition, the soot blackened the trunks so as to render any gray moth resting there very conspicuous and therefore easy prey for a bird.

What happened then is a matter of clear historical record. In the polluted areas, black forms started to replace the grays in nearly 70 species. In some species, such as the Peppered Moth, a number of crucial details are known. Even before the industrial revolution, occasional, very rare, black mutants were found. Such specimens have been preserved in museums, and have been objects of special interest to moth collectors if only because of their rarity and curiosity. Under the new conditions in the forest, however, the black condition, in this instance due to a single dominant gene, began to increase in frequency. The fact that these black mutants are not seen as easily by birds on the black trunks as the original grays was established experimentally. At the present time, in one particular species, moths carrying the gene producing black make up almost 95 percent of the population in the industrially blackened areas. This evolutionary change took place in less than 100 years.[2]

This case is a very instructive example of how a gene with a major effect which is beneficial to the species can be rather quickly established in a natural population by the process of natural selection. The genetic outlines of this case were quite easy to discern because of the rather simple mode of inheritance of the major difference. In some of the species of moths, on the other hand, the mode of inheritance of the black coloration does not seem to be as simple as in the case just described. There seem to be a number of genes involved. It is also interesting that in the case of the Peppered Moth there has been a modification of the degree of dominance of the black color pattern. When the mutation from gray to black first occurred it was not completely dominant and modifying genes have apparently been selected later which make the black coloration of the individual carrying only one dose of the gene more complete.

Natural selection, when applied to the gene pool through individuals, results in the automatic multiplication of good genes, or genes which work well in the particular mode of life in which the living thing finds itself. The process can be closely mimicked by man who has, since the beginning of domestication, practiced artificial selection on the animals and plants which are useful to him. Many of the wonders among our modern argricultural plants owe their existence to the adroit and sharp-eyed intelligence of our forebears, who bred from things close to what they wanted and avoided breeding from the inferior ones.

Evolution, the process which combines descent with hereditary change, is really nothing more complicated than selective breeding. Genetic variations originate wholly by the chance process of mutation and are themselves unrelated to selective breeding. Mutation cannot be directly caused or brought about by any selective agency. The extraordinary progress that has been achieved in the past, as well as the accomplishments of present-day plant and animal breeders, have been made simply by selecting as parents, generation after generation, those animals or plants that embody gene combinations influencing characters in the desired direction.

In order to make progress by selection, it is not necessary to separate the hereditary and environmental components in a character. For example, if one is selecting for body size in dogs, it probably does no harm to select the largest animals for breeding, despite the fact that some of their large size may be due in substantial part to environmental factors such as good feeding. If there is any genetic contribution at all to large size, we are likely to pass along these genes to the next generation and thus make a selective advance. Selection of genes having effects which we want can therefore be effective even if it is blind—blind as to the actual details of the hereditary differences which we are favoring.

This aspect of selection made the process operate well in the hands of our forebears and in the hands of amateurs who were astute observers but nevertheless did not understand just what they were doing. Artificial selection works well in the hands of a perceptive person who knows what he wants and is prepared to be patient, live to a ripe old age himself, and train his children in the same art that he himself has practiced. Speed of advance in selection is limited principally by the length of the generation, that is, the unit of time that it takes to get from the adult stage of one generation to the adult stage of the next.

From what has been said about the relationship between mutation and selection, it is obvious that selection, if no hereditary differences are present on which to operate, is completely ineffective. If no genes have alternatives present, then we are selecting from among identities, which is an obvious absurdity. Various modern methods are now used to ensure that there is always available, to the experimental breeder, a wealth of genetic variability present before selection is begun. In animal and plant breeding, this is most frequently accomplished by making an outcross, that is, a cross between genetically unlike individuals first. One does not ordinarily select from among the first-generation hybrids but rather from among those of the second generation. This permits the full process of genetic recombination to operate, thus producing a large number of diverse genotypes. The ultimate origin of all the variability is, however, the process of mutation itself. Neither selection or recombination are in themselves creative of new variations; they merely produce new combinations of genes which already exist as "raw materials."

Population size

Before going back to a consideration of early human or prehuman populations and applying these principles, we must consider a second factor which affects the rate of evolutionary change very profoundly. This is the size of the population which actually does the breeding, either under natural or artificial selection. This principle may be perhaps best understood by taking an extreme example from artificial selection. Suppose we have a flock of chickens of mixed colors and thoroughly hybridized ancestry. We want, let us say, to select so that our flock will ultimately be composed entirely of red birds. If red is recessive, one type of selective process is very easy; we can merely choose a single red female before she has mated, mate her to a red male, and then breed a whole barnyard of red chickens derived from these two. All the rest of the chickens are then discarded. This sort of result can be accomplished quickly and easily.

The most significant event in the history of the genes of our population of chickens, from the evolutionary point of view, is that our entire population was forced through a single pair of birds by this method of selection. In that key generation when the selection was made, the breeding population was the smallest in size that is possible, namely, one male and one female. One of the things that might happen would be the complete loss, by throwing away so many birds, of genes leading to other colors or perhaps even to desirable characters like heavy weight and the ability to lay a large number of eggs. Conversely, the two red birds that you select might, just by chance, have double doses for some other genes which are quite separate from the red for which they were chosen. This gene or gene combination might have a bad effect. It might be, for example, a gene which decreases the average number of eggs laid, produces crooked toes, increases proneness to infection, or otherwise decreases vigor.

This will mean that selection, either natural or artificial, which utilizes very small populations runs the risk of fixing permanently, in all of the descendants, certain bad genes as well as those which are the object of the selection itself. Running a population through bottlenecks like this has the effect of drastically altering gene frequencies from generation to generation. In our example, the gene for black chickens might have been present at about 25 percent before we ran the population through two birds. In the new flock, the gene for black would have been completely eliminated.

Every time a natural population is for any reason forced through a narrow bottleneck of population size, such as a small migrant group reaching and populating an uninhabited island, there is likely to be important genetic change from the ancestral situation. This will be due to the fact that the population is rebuilt from a small sample of the hereditary material of the original population. This sample may to some extent represent only a chance sample from the original gene pool. When it is expanded again, the gene composition of this new pool is different from that of the one from which it came. The fate of this new gene pool depends upon how strictly isolated it may be from other gene pools close to it in a geographical sense. If there is a lot of migration back and forth, so-called gene flow between adjacent gene pools, these two pools, as described in a previous chapter, will not remain separate but will themselves slowly become one. On the other hand, if a new gene pool, after the bottlenecking process and its accompanied genetic change, remains seperate and isolated, is relatively inbred, and under strong selection, the initial divergence may not only be retained but intensified.[3]

The interplay of these evolutionary factors, especially mutation rate, selection rate, and population size changes, as expressed in changes in gene frequency in populations, can be treated mathematically. From such calculations, it can be shown that the ideal situation for really fast evolution exists in relatively small populations which are semi-isolated in the sense that they are subjected to rather intense selection and inbreeding but occasionally receive a small number of migrants from adjacent populations.

To state this in a slightly different way: Isolation, close inbreeding, and selection in small populations leads to relative genetic uniformity among members of the population which has had this treatment. Correspondingly, such populations become different from geographically separate ones in which similar events are occurring. Genetic variability may become exhausted, selection rendered ineffective because there are no genetic differences left to select from. Either a continuing high mutation rate or occasional immigration of individuals from adjacent populations would, on the other hand, continue to furnish a source of gene variability. It would also prevent the permanent and complete isolation of such a gene pool.

Human evolution, like that of all other living things which have a system of heredity similar to that of the human, has been the result of the interplay of these processes. Two of the processes, mutation and recombination of genes, are governed almost wholly by the laws of chance. Natural selection, population size changes, and degree of isolation of gene pools are governed by the positive and explicit requirements of the environment in which the population finds itself.

The manner in which man evolved

We can now make an attempt to explain the nature and origin of the early gene pools of the human species from subhuman ancestral populations. The two features of importance to be borne in mind are that the evolution was rapid and that it involved almost entirely one key organ, namely, the brain.

All the evidence indicates that the most important prehuman ancestors of man must have been rather small-bodied, upright forms living in grasslands or forest edges in southern Africa, about a million and a half years ago. They probably existed in relatively small semi-isolated populations or in small family groups which were somewhat migratory, living on small game, birds, and fish, but able to consume vegetable food as well.

Lacking as they did any specialization of limbs or teeth or sense organs, food-gathering in these groups quite likely became associated with a type of mental activity wholly unique among living things. First, there is the acute perception of the minute details of a food-yielding situation, even if those details may not have seemed relevant at the moment. These details reappear in the mind as applied to a new situation, correlations are made, and conclusions, the bases for intelligent action, are reached.

Each new situation is solved in terms of past experience, but the conditioned or stereotyped response is supplemented and to a large extent replaced by sensitivity, selection, and cumulative flexibility of decision. The second important ingredient of this situation is the ability not only to apply this situation to one's own individual problems, but, by communication, to provide the group with the benefits of experience as well. Furthermore, a new bridge between the generations can be built which comes to be of an even greater importance in the human species than the biological bridge of egg and sperm. This is the acquisition of a new type of inheritance, cultural inheritance, wherein the individuals of one generation teach, by precept and by word, the experience of their own and past groups to those of the younger generation.

Among the rather small populations of australopithecine nearmen, we may surmise that natural selection at first favored genes which resulted in improved ability of the brain to cope with the matter of daily requirements of food, shelter, and care of young. This may sound like an obvious statement of a principle which might equally apply to other evolving animal groups such as monkeys or horses or cats. The difference, of course, lies in the way the brain was used. Intelligence of the human sort appears to depend on certain very complex configurations of cells in the brain. We are unable to look at a brain structure and identify certain features as important for intelligence in the way that we can look at the forefoot of a mole and diagnose the biological significance of this structure in the natural selection of the mole. Because human intelligence has no gross structural manifestation, except possibly the existence of the speech center and general brain size, we cannot look at the reconstructed brain of a fossil form and specify the exact degree of intelligent behavior that he must have possessed.

Despite these difficulties, however, we have no hesitation in stating that human evolution is almost completely the history of the evolution of the capacity for culture, as we have specified above. When looked upon in this way, some of the puzzles of the rapidity of human evolution may be explained. When natural selection begins to favor gene changes having to do with one particular organ, say, the shovel-like form of the mole forelimb, there is very good evidence that evolution can be very fast when this organ has reached the stage when the advantage to the reproduction of the mole (through much more efficient gathering of its principal food, earthworms) suddenly becomes really substantial. Accumulation of gene changes may suddenly seem to "snowball."

Previously, such a rapid phase of evolution was thought to be due to the occurrence of one or two "lucky" mutations which immediately provided a big new service. Genetic analysis of such characters, however, shows that their genetic basis frequently consists of many genes, each of which appears to make only a modest contribution to the character. We can only conclude that the character must have been built up piece by piece, as it has been shown mathematically that it is virtually impossible for selection to deal with more than one gene at the same time.

This brings us to the crux of the situation with respect to the evolution of a human brain with the capacity for developing cultural traditions. As natural selection came to favor gene changes in brain structure leading to flexibility of mind, these changes found themselves being incorporated into very small gene pools, representing the family or clanlike organization of early prehuman populations. It should be emphasized here that this kind of population structure is only presumed; there is no independent evidence which indicates just what the nature of these prehuman populations was. Every inference from the structure of descendant populations, however, leads us to the conclusion that the populations had indeed very small effective sizes. Within small, semi-isolated, and somewhat inbred gene pools, selection could push mutations favoring human brain structure quite quickly to high frequency. Accordingly, we can visualize prehuman populations of the early Pleistocene as having arrived at a crucial stage of size and social organization that was especially favorable to the rapid evolution of the higher mental faculties.

When we contemplate the fossil record, we are often struck by the enormous expanses of time, involving millions of generations, over which evolutionary events have apparently occurred. What is to some degree hidden from us is the very uneven rate at which events of great importance proceed. In short, evolution occurs in fits and starts. When an animal or plant has achieved a genetic condition enabling it to really master an environmental situation, it may then spread over continents and perhaps develop vast numerical superiority. Such sudden conquest of new areas, with its attendant vast populations, commonly occurs only after the acquisition of new adaptive features which make the spread possible. The spread is possible because of the evolutionary event that has preceded it. The features enabling the spread are themselves rarely changed much or even perfected during the period of wide distribution.

Evolutionists have perhaps emphasized too much the slowness of evolution. We are only now coming to realize just what the prerequisites for rapid evolution are. In the present connection, the important application to the human case is that the genetic basis of the human brain as we know it could indeed have evolved in considerably less time than the million years of the Pleistocene; we need no recourse to the 20 to 40 times that amount of time which has been sometimes suggested as being necessary.

By a time approximately 40,000 years ago, the evolution of the brain as we know it was essentially complete, and the conquest of the corners of the world by the new human species, armed with this sensitive and unprecedented evolutionary achievement, began. The source populations were surely from North Africa, southern Europe, or the Middle East, but, as they went, they carried with them the same close, bandlike, but not completely closed, population structure that was such an important welding device for the evolutionary millennia of the Pleistocene. For a relatively very brief period, perhaps 35,000 years, human populations carried this same semi-isolated structure. The events that occurred during this brief moment of history, the formation of the groups we recognize as the geographical races of mankind, with their accompanying different cultural inheritances as well, will concern us in the next chapter.

Summary

The raw materials of evolution are the gene changes, that is, mutations, but the fate of these is determined primarily by the all-prevading force of natural selection. Selection determines whether a newly arisen gene, which may be carried at first by only a few individuals in the gene pool, will become more frequent in the gene pool or will be eliminated. If the gene serves to aid the person who carries it by increasing the efficiency with which numerous and healthy offspring are produced, its frequency will increase in the gene pool. The essence of selection is differential reproduction, of which survival is only a part.

Small, semi-isolated natural populations are the most efficient for rapid evolution and it is suggested that early prehuman populations were of this type, being band or clanlike, providing the best opportunity for the rapid evolution of a brain having the capacity for culture, a development which is unique in nature. The spread of man over the continents, his great numerical increase, and his cultural and genetic subdivision into geographical races are exceedingly recent events, on the order of 40,000 years. It has been accompanied by little fundamental genetic change.

Chapter 9

ISOLATION AND RACE
FORMATION

Prehistoric migrations

MAN was man when the great migrations began. These migrations carried him from an apparently localized geographical origin to every corner of the globe. He went down into the continent of Africa; he went through Europe north to the Lappland fringes. Migrants crossed Asia, embarked into the South Seas, reaching Australia, New Zealand, and Tasmania. They went northeast through China and Manchuria to Bering Strait, into America, and thence south all the way to Tierra del Fuego.

What was certainly a numerically rather insignificant ancestral group formed the base population from which all modern men have come. Every evidence indicates that this spreading of the human species in prehistoric times took place with only the most primitive methods of travel and proceeded stepwise from one geographical point to the next. Most important of all, however, is the fact that Columbus did not discover America any more than Captain Cook discovered Australia; both were perhaps 30,000 years later than the real discoverers.

During this period of migration and colonization, before the beginning of recorded human history, the races of man were formed. As we have seen, this is a very brief period, amounting to a mere 30,000 years, approximately 1,000 generations. This is the first time that the word race has been used and it is important to make clear what this term means in technical biological usage. A race is simply one of the partially isolated gene pools into which the human species came to be divided during and following its early geographical spread. Roughly one race has developed on each of the five major continental areas of the earth; North and South America may be considered as one continent for this purpose. If we adopt this "one continent, one race" concept as an aid to our thinking, it must be recognized that within each of the continents and on adjacent islands there exist hundreds of possible further minor subdivisions. Indeed, some race-classifiers tend to apply the term to each small, partially isolated gene pool that can be recognized within continents or on isolated islands. As a result, dozens or even hundreds of races may be recognized, depending on the attitude of the classifier. Such "splitting" in classification need not concern those who wish to take the broad view of the situation, although the formation of the subgroups is an interesting and important problem in itself.

For example, the Americas were populated by migrants who arrived from Asia by the land-bridge over Bering Strait early (perhaps 25,000 years ago) in the history of human distribution. The broad scheme of classification would put them and all their descendants in the Amerind (American Indian) race. Such a classification does not deny or render unimportant the fact that American Indians are further subdivided. They indeed are, but when viewing the world picture as a whole it is unnecessary to take such details into account.

Two other facts render rigid, detailed classification schemes unwieldy and, in fact, almost useless. The first is that the continental areas where the major subdivisions of the human gene pool took place were never in fact completely isolated for a mobile species like man, even in prehistoric times. Some, of course, like

Australia and New Zealand, were more isolated than others, but in point of fact Asia, Europe, and Africa, in particular, had land routes connecting them all through the crucial period when the races were being formed. This meant of course that populations were frequently continuous from one continental race into another. This resulted in intervening populations which to some degree showed intermediacy and therefore were and still are not easily classifiable with one or another of the continental races. "Bridge" populations of this sort have probably always existed since the earliest days of widespread distribution.

Second, within each continental race, considerable variability exists from subgroup to subgroup, as has been mentioned earlier. Accordingly, it is not possible, from the biological point of view, to draw up a description of a "typical" member or even subgroup of any race. In fact, populations are not made up of types but rather groups of genetically different individuals, no two of which are alike. Thus, one can characterize the Amerind race, for example, only in very general terms. To present as a "typical representative of an Amerind" a picture of an individual Naskapi, Sioux, Chocó, or Fuegan is obviously absurd. It is almost equally meaningless to try to substitute some sort of population measure if it represents some arbitrary choice of a subgroup as "typical." From the biological point of view, every single minor subdivision of Amerind is just as significant as any other and none has any inherent biological superiority because of its past history, genetic properties, or geographical position. This statement, of course, does not deny the existence of differences between groups or the importance of being in a key geographical position for the eventual development of large population size, complex culture, and political power.

The process of race formation by a newly formed, rapidly spreading, and successful species is well known and has been the subject of a great deal of investigation on species other than man.

ISOLATION AND RACE FORMATION

We may apply these principles to man and make the following surmises. As a small population becomes larger because of the success of its members, it requires more space in which to live and moves easily into that space. Pressures of food-getting, particularly, result in a gradual extension of boundaries of distribution, generation by generation. In the case of the human species, with a brain which is capable of fear, joy, hope, and imagination, as well as keen perception, the idea of an El Dorado beyond the horizon certainly helped to keep men moving from one area to another. This can be coupled with the fact that early human societies were mostly simple hunting and fishing ones. Occupations such as these preceded the more sedentary existence that followed the development of agriculture.

As we contemplate the teeming populations of the present century, it is hard to imagine the way in which these prehistoric populations must have been organized. It is likely that each new area was reached and colonized by a relatively small band of individuals which then settled down for a number of generations to exploit and occupy the new region in relatively great isolation from adjacent groups (Chapter 6). The clan, band, or tribe, or whatever name connotes a semi-isolated unit of small size, was the unit which corresponded to the smallest subdivision of the gene pool as each new area was reached.

As successive waves of migration and movement of peoples occurred, the clan structure was essentially preserved. During the phase of race formation, there is considerable evidence that a high degree of isolation was maintained between the units, starting at the continental unit and extending all the way down to the local clan. A unit settling in an area would be quite likely to resist occupation of the same area by another similar band. This second band would be likely to bypass such an occupied area and move on, thus continuing and speeding up the spread of the species as a whole.

The very closely knit band, once it settles in an area, becomes ever more united by custom and culture and forms just the type of small semi-isolated population which permits the rapid accumulation of differences, both genetic and cultural, within it. Man did indeed diverge genetically during this phase of history and we can measure and study the results of this divergence in what remains today of the old geographical races. As we would expect, divergence appears to be correlated with the degree of isolation. Those peoples who populated the extreme margins of the habitable areas of the continents, Terra del Fuego, Baffin Island, or Tasmania had extreme geographical isolation as well as the obligatory small populations that accompany the harsh and adverse living conditions found in such marginal areas. Thus, within each of the five major continental geographical races, a great abundance of small local populations was formed during this crucial stage in the growth of the world's human population.

Isolation and its genetic consequences

Isolation, however, is not conditioned by geographical distance alone; it can take other forms. Pygmy tribes, for example, of which a number of quite separate instances are known, exist (or existed) within certain of the continental races. These consist of people who isolated themselves effectively even when geographically ringed by nonpygmy groups. Actually, the genetic basis of the pygmy condition is not very complex; relatively few genes are involved. Indeed, many other strongly isolated groups, such as the Basques of Spain, were equally as effectively isolated and show no less a degree of genetic divergence, even though it may not take the spectacular form of short stature.

All early human societies showed some degree of isolation. Both the Australian continent and the Western Hemisphere were occupied by a veritable crazy quilt of peoples, each maintaining themselves in a state of more or less stringent isolation. These extraordinary isolations have in some instances persisted right to the present day. In the interior of New Guinea, for instance, where isolation is aided by rugged mountains, a small group of villages will form an almost completely isolated unit with its own language, culture, and customs. There are still in existence nearly 500 such isolated units on this single relatively small land mass.

The factors which operated between two adjacent clans or tribes are almost precisely the same factors that still continue to operate, to some degree, in modern populations. People tend to marry not only those who are close to them in their environment but, human social organization being what it is, factors of origin, cultural background, religion, and family pressures of one sort or another tend to channel marriages along certain lines, usually keeping them within a certain group.

Small populations of all sorts tend to accumulate genetic differences and man is no exception. The differences which accumulate under such conditions are not necessarily directly related to the dictates of natural selection. Selection has unquestionably been instrumental in molding the present form of the human species, but it is easy to overemphasize its importance. For example, if the genetic basis of a character is present in a living thing, this fact is sometimes loosely used as evidence that selection must have strongly favored it in the past. This is not necessarily true. When selection favors one gene, especially in small populations, other genes may be "carried along" with the one which is being selected. In this way, some genes can become established even though they themselves may tend to reduce the fitness of the individuals in the gene pool of which they have become a part. Under other circumstances and in larger populations, selection might have rejected them and eliminated them from the population.

Such "carried-along" effects are encountered repeatedly in experimental animal and plant breeding where it is necessary, in most cases, to use quite small populations for breeding purposes. For instance, in selecting dog breeds, man pays particular attention to characters of personality, color, hair form, and shape of head and limbs. In each generation the animals are run through a bottleneck of a few individuals; this process sets the stage for carrying along, merely by chance, genes which produce other effects which sometimes represent a loss in fitness, such as poor eyesight or impaired reproductive efficiency. Just as striking is the frequent incidental carrying along of genes leading to completely odd characters, such as whether the tail curves up or down and whether or not muscles which can cock the ears are present. This is the random drift effect in small populations; it has previously been described in Chapter 6.

It seems very likely that most genetic differences apparent between groups of mankind are not there because of the dictates of selection for different life conditions, but rather are due to the operation of chance genetic events in small populations. Since it first became apparent that natural selection was important in explaining evolution, this concept has been used to explain human differences. Much has been made, for example, of the supposed adaptive nature of dark skin in tropical areas, of the short stature, facial features, and certain fat distribution in arctic peoples, and so on. The hypothesis that these differences were established by natural selection as the races were formed, however attractive it may be, is not well supported by study of the characters concerned. In short, no very strong evidence exists that even the most suggestive characters are in fact adaptive.

Even the most ardent proponents of the view that selection has established these differences must admit that a number of minor differences from one group to the next, such as skin color, eye color and shape, ear shape, hair texture and degree of curliness, stature, body build, shape of fingers and toes, and so on, require the adaptation-by-selection hypothesis to be stretched too far.

How, then, do we escape the paradox that selection, which certainly has been a major guiding force in evolution, appears not to have been so important in the origin of the genetic differences between the different racial groups? In the writer's opinion, the solution lies in two phenomena: the brief time that the races have existed (1,000 generations) and the effects of random drift in small populations.

According to this view, man, following his origin, did not undergo much direct selection for body characteristics that fitted him into any particular environment or provided for any specific environmental needs, such as climate and geography would appear to demand. The brain, already perfected before the migrations, had equipped this new species with intelligence, a powerful new instrument of survival of transcendent importance. It provided man with a means of coping with specific situations which had never been encountered in the entire history of the species.

Nevertheless, a thousand generations of existence in small populations would provide ample opportunity for superficial genetic differences to become incorporated into the separated gene pools. Once they exist, moreover, and find themselves a part of the daily scene, conspicuous superficial differences may find themselves entering into the concept of physical beauty or "rightness" which the isolated group develops as part of its culture. Such concepts may, in those early isolates, have had a very great influence on who was and who was not encouraged, or indeed permitted, to participate in reproduction. This state of affairs could have resulted in a sort of secondary selection based on a cultural, psychological need.

In this view, then, man has selectively bred himself in a rather haphazard fashion for 30,000 years or so in thousands of isolates within the five major land masses of the earth. We recognize the result in the physical diversity of man.

Group differences

As has been stressed earlier, individual hereditary differences are a matter of gene differences. By the same token, group differences in heredity must be described in terms of the differences in frequencies of recognizable genes. To describe the hereditary essence of a group in this way, however, is an extraordinarily difficult matter in the human species because almost every character of importance has a strong environmental, that is, cultural, component. The problem is made easier by describing only group differences in characters which have little environmental ingredient, such as the chemical differences in blood. Such studies provide mathematical and statistical means for distinguishing groups.

The amateur who enters the field of judging group differences makes many mistakes, two of which are especially bad. Because he has no means to observe such things as chemical differences and because his experience is not wide enough, he has no basis for distinguishing the environmental and hereditary components of a character that he sees. The result is a confused view which opens the way for a facile overestimation of either heredity or environment, depending on the bias of the observer. Second, all observations, of course, must be initially made on individuals, and no intuitive or easy way exists for comparing two groups each of which is made up of dissimilar individuals. The amateur frequently escapes from this dilemma by ascribing to *groups* characteristics which properly pertain only to *individuals.*

As variability within almost every human group is very great, the amateur's comparisons are, except in a few conspicuous characters, meaningless. For instance, he may venture the generalization that "Irish have red hair and Fijians have black hair," whereas actual counts will show many black-haired Irish and red-haired Fijians. The only way out is to specify the frequency of the genes within the two gene pools. Before this can be done, the details of the mode of inheritance of the character must be known and the frequency determinations on both islands made by someone who is fully aware of complicating factors such as the use of hair dyes.

In recent years, a large amount of very valuable data on the frequency of various genes in different human gene pools has been collected. The most useful measurements, of course, are of characters, like the blood groups or hemoglobin types, which are chemical ones, hidden from view, and having a simple hereditary basis. Characters such as these cannot be changed by the person having them, in fact, he is normally unaware of them; determination of them does not require an elaborate test or the employment of subjective judgments.

It should be remembered, however, that when we record differences like these and compare gene pools on such a basis, we are actually identifying only one of hundreds of gene loci, the description and frequency of which would be necessary if we were to describe the hereditary components of the group satisfactorily. A particular race or subgroup cannot be described only in terms of blood-group genes; these protein differences are of no greater significance as bases for separation than any other superficial character with an hereditary basis, such as the width of the nasal septum.

Although we have been able to identify and study the frequency of only a few genes in human gene pools, the sound scientific data which they provide allow us to see, in dim outline, the shape of genetic differences between human groups. The essential feature is that most of the genes studied prove to be present in most of the races. Races, therefore, differ principally in displaying various intermediate gene frequencies, not in whether the gene is universally present or absent in the gene pools being compared.

Up to this point, we have not discussed genetic differences in mental capacity and posed the question of the extent to which such differences may exist between groups. This is probably the most important question of all because everyone knows that the measure of a man is not his external appearance or the coagulation properties of his blood but elusive characters of his brain, his intellectual capacity and his capacity for human warmth and understanding.

Individual genetic components in these characters exist within groups; this has been documented in the chapter on heredity and environment. The twin studies, in particular, enable us to recognize the fact that genes are involved to a considerable extent in all sorts of mental differences, but we cannot identify particular genes, primarily because the environmental effects on the same characters are so strong. Therefore, the gene-frequency method of comparing groups cannot be applied to mental traits in the way it has been used for blood groups or other hereditary differences with simpler genetic bases. Thus we are unable to apply the new, precise methods to this crucial area. Nevertheless, what we now know about human biology enables us to make surmises which surely are closer to the truth than the wild guesses and emotional declamations of the past.

Genetic and cultural inheritance

The genes that each of us get are obtained at the moment of fertilization. Our genetic inheritance is fixed from that moment forward and cannot be changed. On the other hand, environmental influence begins at the moment of fertilization and continues throughout the life of the individual.

Man differs from other forms of life in having a type of brain which is able to maximize the importance of environmental influences. When we are born, we find ourselves within a group which has developed in a partial isolation; our group has a set of traditions and influences that are all-pervading. As soon as a baby's eyes are open, he starts to learn from those that are older, that is, the previous generation. All the values, attitudes, methods of doing things, mode of speech, type of clothing, ways of walking, and so on are learned from elders. The culture of the group demands conformism; in both subtle and brutal ways, the learning process continues during every waking moment.

The learning process in man forms a bridge between the generations which in many ways has come to transcend the importance of the narrow hereditary bridge based on the genes. It is really another type of inheritance; we may call it cultural inheritance. Genetic inheritance is based on transmission of information in the form of DNA from one generation to the next; it is a gene to gene process. Cultural inheritance is based on transmission of information by a teaching-learning mechanism from one generation to the next; it is a brain to brain process. Cultural inheritance is indeed an environmental influence so strong as to introduce a whole new and difficult dimension. Some human qualities seem so firmly entrenched that they seem to be inherent, coming from the genes, whereas they are in fact learned; they are part of the culture.

Both genetic and cultural inheritance have fundamental and far-reaching influences on the ultimate behavior of the individual. In fact, perhaps the most important attribute of the human brain is its ability to accept cultural inheritance, that is, to learn. Genetic differences in brains may interfere with this process. For example, certain genes or gene combinations may lead to idiocy, feeble-mindedness, schizophrenia, or other major mental disorders. When this happens, cultural inheritance is greatly impaired and becomes uneven. The whole teaching-learning process is likely to be incomplete despite heroic efforts of teachers. The most important fact here is that cultural inheritance fails and the failure is directly attributable to the genetic deficiency of the receiving mind.

Every gene-pool subdivision as it was formed acquired a different culture. Each has its own unique combination of skills and superstitions, its reasoning and unreasoning attitudes, its all-pervading demands for uniformity through conformity. This is a great deal for even so remarkable an instrument as the human brain to handle.

When race formation took place on the continents, with the bottlenecking of thousands of populations in isolated gene pools all over the world, the gene-frequency differences we now see were established. As emphasized earlier, most of the gene-frequency differences which we term racial (skin and hair color, stature, facial characteristics) apparently were established more or less by chance. Later, perhaps, they became part of concepts of beauty and thus were favored by selection.

Comparable differences in brains could not have been established in this way. The brain has been from the very beginning the major genetic instrument which enabled *Homo sapiens* to be so successful. Any small-population effects which may have affected gene frequencies leading to a high frequency of poorly operating minds would have spelled the extinction of the group.

Certain structures tend to take the lead as adaptation occurs. The main evolutionary force, natural selection, will build them rapidly into instruments of high efficiency. Every chance gene change which favors better function is built into the population by selection and is brought to a high frequency. Both mole arm and human brain were originally molded in this way. As each species spread geographically and broke into isolated populations, small population effects might tamper with superficial and unimportant characters such as the shape of the mole's tail or the color of a man's skin. Genetic alteration of the prime instrument of survival, however, does not happen when a successful species spreads and forms races. In the human case, we are aware that genetic variation affecting the brain's fundamental ability arises continually and there is ample evidence of variation of this sort within many existing populations. The point is, however, that such genes have never become so frequent anywhere as to characterize the gene pool of the group in the way that the genes leading to certain skin colors and facial and bodily features have. Nature can tamper with superficial characteristics in small drifting populations but it cannot, without courting extinction, discard the major organ on which survival rests. Stupidity is, in fact, far less tenable in a Stone Age culture than it is in a modern urban one.

The paradox which faces us is that each group of humans appears to be externally different yet underneath these differences these is fundamental similarity. How can men be the same and different simultaneously? Simply, it is because the evolution of the brain occurred before the superficial racial divergence.

Each original continental subdivision of man has a broad range of gene variability affecting the brain. Although methods exist for assessing this variability within groups, we still cannot estimate the variability between groups with any scientific accuracy. Yet it seems safe at our present state of knowledge to say that any group differences, if such can be recognized in the future, would be so minor as to be wholly insignificant.

Even if certain genes leading to brains capable of performing the highest intellectual functions were somewhat more frequent in one group than another, this would not significantly affect the position of the millions of genotypes which lie between the extremes. Variation in ultimate performance, even if genetically based, should not be allowed to blind us to the deep similarities that run below the surface. Every normal man has a brain which reacts with delicate sensitivity, which desires dignity and trust, which displays at once a strong measure of basic intelligence and deep emotional warmth. These qualities lead to common aspirations. When shunted into abnormality, by whatever combination of causes, there can be no tragedy greater, no menace to mankind more severe, than the twisted or broken mind.

Summary

After his evolution as a species, man spread relatively quickly to all parts of the earth. This was made possible because of the flexibility of his mentality, the genetic basis of which had evolved prior to his geographical spread. Genetic divergence accompanying this spread resulted in the formation of about five major subdivisions of the human gene pool called races. At the beginning of historic time, each race was in turn subdivided into thousands of semi-isolated tribes or clans among which further genetic divergence occurred. The most important biological aspect of these early human populations was their tendency to originate from a few migrants and then to remain in strong but not complete isolation from each other. The effect of the original bottlenecking of population size promoted the chance divergence of groups with respect to frequencies of genes affecting many superficial characters, such as skin and hair color, facial features, and body build. At the clan, or local population level, characters of this sort may enter into the concept of orthodoxy or beauty of the group and thus the genes underlying these characters are subject to a capricious selection of secondary importance. The gene pool of each major race, subdivided as it was into a mosaic of semi-isolated minor gene pools, differs from the other races in the frequency of certain genes. Only rarely are certain genes completely absent in one race and completely fixed, that is, present in 100 percent of individuals, in another race. This is shown especially well in a number of hereditary characters of a biochemical sort, such as blood groups and hemoglobins.

The evidence indicates that while external variation between races may be great in superficial characters like skin color, hereditary variation between groups in basic brain function is at most very slight. Man's brain is the primary organ which permitted his success. It operates by permitting a new type of transfer of information from generation to generation. In addition to the biological inheritance, represented by the DNA of the reproductive cells, man's brain is such that it permits cultural inheritance. Once the capacity for cultural inheritance was established genetically by the evolution of the brain, evolution of behavior characteristics within groups can proceed without much basic genetic change. The existence of a powerful cultural inheritance makes the separation of the hereditary and environmental contributions to a given behavioral trait exceedingly difficult to measure. Cultural inheritance, to work well, requires that most of the individuals of the group concerned have complex, delicately balanced, and efficient brains. Every human group gives evidence of a high frequency of genes leading to this result. Thus we have the paradox of geographical isolates, races, showing marked physical differences as groups but not showing mental differences of comparable magnitude. Men are different, but at the same time are alike. This is apparently the outcome of the fact that during the formation of races natural selection would not permit the establishment of groups with high gene frequencies leading to brains which functioned poorly in cultural inheritance. High frequency of stupidity would have been untenable in any human group. Great hereditary variability in mental capacity exists within each of the surviving separate human populations. Nevertheless, the last 40,000 years of human history have seen very little differential isolation and accumulation, within racial or tribal confines, of genes which form the very basis of man's unique quality, his capacity for culture.

Chapter 10

THE HISTORIC BREAKDOWN OF ISOLATION

The single human species

ALL men living on the earth today, and all those who have lived for at least 40,000 years back of the present belong to one biological species, *Homo sapiens*. A species is best defined as that group of living things belonging to the same interbreeding group. Thus, if two individuals of the opposite sex are capable of being mutually attracted, of performing the sex act, and subsequently of rearing normal offspring which are themselves fully fertile, we may assign all these individuals to the same species.

A world-wide species like the human one is made up of millions of individuals. Our basis for judging these all to be the same species is the fact that successful interbreeding has occurred in many instances between even the most dissimilar races. Thus we conclude that the degree of biological difference between the members of existing human groups is not as great as that which is found between biological species.

This consideration of successful interbreeding not only serves to define just what is meant by the term species but also points up the fact that the edge of the species is identical with the edge of the gene pool. In this case, we are referring to the major or species gene pool. Up to this point in the discussion we have emphasized that the various local or racial gene pools are separated from one another by incomplete barriers of one kind or another. Thus each local gene pool can receive at least a minor amount of gene flow from adjacent semi-isolated ones. The boundary between the major gene pools of two separate species is different from the above because it is an absolute boundary across which no interbreeding, or gene flow, occurs.

The use of the interbreeding criterion for the recognition of species must be based on the observation of many cases, because within all biological species, abnormal conditions leading to sterility or some other sort of reproductive failure may occur. Thus it is necessary to distinguish between lack of reproduction by a couple for some pathological reason and failure by reason of some basic biological difference of an evolutionary nature between the potential reproductive partners. Between the groups of individuals of two different species, then, there is an unbridgeable gap across which no gene flow is possible. When this point in the history of two gene pools is reached, the destiny of each pool becomes irrevocably separate, even though the two may have originally had a common ancestry.

Before considering humans specifically, let us examine how the unbridgeable gap is manifested in various animal cases. The horse and the ass are quite different animals but clearly show a strong evolutionary relationship, like man and chimpanzee. The horse is Asiatic and the ass is African. Are they different races of the same species or are they different species? When horse is crossed to ass, the result is the mule, which, despite its vigor, is sterile. The sterile hybrid individual has a permanent reproductive disability; he derives this condition from the mutual incompatibility of the genetic material of his two parents. There thus exists a barrier between the gene pools from which his two parents were drawn. In this case, it is represented by the failure of the hybrid to pass his genes on at all. Flow down through the generations stops with him and the pools remain separate. Races can flow back together again because interracial hybrids are fully fertile; species cannot flow together because the sterility of the hybrids keeps them apart.

Separation of the gene pools of two species may be maintained in other ways. First, as in the case of the cat and dog, the males and females may show no interest sexually in one another under any circumstances. Thus, even if a cross-fertilized egg could be formed, the possibility of gene exchange between the populations from which the two individuals come is blocked because the cells can never meet. In other animal cases which have been studied, mating between the two may occur freely, as in the horse-ass case, but no offspring are produced. This may be due to immobilization of the sperm even before it reaches the egg, or, if it reaches the egg, there may be some incompatibility between the two cells. In still other cases, the egg may be fertilized and the embryo may grow vigorously only to be regularly lost by miscarriage during the gestation period.

In none of the cases cited above could genes flow from one group into the other. Two such groups could, in fact often do, actually live in the same geographical area and yet maintain complete genetic isolation. Borderline cases of new species just in the process of formation are known. In such cases, the hybrid offspring of one sex (often the male) are sterile but those of the opposite sex are fertile if crossed back to an individual from one of the parental gene pools. Situations of very great complexity have been uncovered in studies of this sort in certain animals and in many plants. These are particularly interesting because of the light which they throw on the nature and origin of gaps between species.

It is of particular interest and relevance to our discussion to inquire whether crosses between human beings of dissimilar racial origin show evidence of any such genetic incompatibilities. One of the greatest difficulties encountered in human genetics is that unlike the animal cases, matings can never be arranged specifically to answer the important questions that the geneticist would like to pose. We must seek out matings of the kind desired and study them. Most fortunately, interracial crosses in man have occurred frequently and abundantly. Under the impact of the world-wide human movements of the historic era, especially during the period of the great European voyages, crosses of almost every sort have occurred.

The results of these natural experiments are clear and simple. There is no evidence, despite ample opportunity for it to show up, of genetic incompatibility of any sort. There are no human sterile hybrids. In fact, individuals having parents of different racial backgrounds are in no way unusual in any biological features. On the whole, they do not appear to be any more or less vigorous and healthy than individuals whose parents came from the same gene-pool subdivision. From the point of view of body structure, pigmentation, facial features, and so forth, the product of an interracial cross tends to be on the whole intermediate between his parents; this is true also for children of parents who are more closely related.

What has been said about interracial crosses does not contradict or change the fact that cultural differences between persons of different racial backgrounds are great and are important factors in the continuing semi-isolation of the races from one another. Emotional isolation, isolation by mental and physical symbols, indeed, all cultural isolation, has always been very strong between groups, but it has no genetic basis. This is shown by the fully compatible and concordant biological reproduction which can ensue if circumstances succeed in bypassing the cultural blocks.

Summarizing, then, we may say that every man and woman now living on earth belongs to a single biological species, *Homo sapiens*. This species acquired its gap from preexisting or related coexisting species, as we have seen previously, about 40,000 years ago. Shortly after its formation, our species probably had quite a small population. As the species enlarged and spread, the geographical semi-isolates, the races, were formed. The gene pools of these races had become further divided into a very large number of local gene pools represented by clans, tribes, religious sects, or village communities.

This tendency towards localization and compartmentalization of the human gene pool was very strong up to the beginning of historic times, when this trend stopped. The barriers to gene flow, so great at that time, fell away somewhat, although not with any uniformity or predictability. Simultaneously with the breakdown of some isolations, other new ones developed, whereas still others held the ancient intact line. Viewed broadly, however, the recorded history of man is essentially a record of the breakdown of the old isolations in all parts of the world. These will be considered in more detail later.

Although man retains to this day myriads of partially separated gene pools, the essential fact is that unbridgeable species gaps never appeared between any of these isolated human groups, even between those isolated the longest. If the separations had been more complete and more fundamental biologically, that is, if the differences accumulated had involved something more than superficial bodily characteristics, a mosaic of hundreds of separate species might have been formed, although the best biological indications are that far more time than 40,000 years would have been required for such a process to be completed

The process of race formation is widely acknowledged to be an essential initial step which sets the stage for the formation of new species. The human species took a dramatic step in this direction through the formation of clearly defined geographical races, but the trend was reversed before the crucial stage was reached.

There is no natural rule or law which requires that an evolutionary process or tendency, once begun, must proceed inexorably toward any foreordained state. In nature, it is only man's mind that preconceives. All we can say, then, is that although a number of new species might indeed have been carved out from parts of *Homo sapiens,* no such species were formed. On the contrary, during the last 5,000 years the tendency has been for the earlier semi-isolations to break down rather than intensify.

Gene and cultural flow

The height of the "crazy quilt" stage of human separation was reached somewhere between 10,000 and 5,000 years ago. No single event or time can be singled out as heralding the coming reversal of the previous trend. Even when isolation was the greatest, however, it was never complete. A small number of migrants promoting interbreeding between adjacent semi-isolates in all likelihood kept open a small flow of genes across the continents, through the islands, and into the remotest areas.

This gene flow, even though quite minor, had the effect of maintaining genetic variability within the isolated populations. It is a remarkable fact that only a very little migration of genetic material from the outside is sufficient to raise the genetic variability of the recipient group, and keep it high. This is probably the main explanation for the fact that even in the most highly inbred and isolated clans or tribes a surprising amount of genetic variability can be shown to be present. An exceedingly small number of intergroup crosses would be all that is necessary to explain the situation.

The process of gene flow between even rather distant groups may be very indirect. Genes may slowly work their way through quite strong isolations by stepwise progress. For instance, prior to the Roman era let us assume the existence of five aboriginal populations in Europe, occupying the contiguous areas A, B, C, D, and E from, let us say, the Baltic to the Mediterranean. Under the influence of strong local isolation, each of these may have acquired a gene pool which differed from the others in the frequencies of a number of genes. Even without massive migration or crossing between single individuals of A and B, however, the gene pools can remain in contact by exchange at their borders. This exchange of genes, even though not condoned by the culture of the groups concerned, may occasionally take place just at those points where one group comes in contact with the next. Under these circumstances, genes from group A could make their way slowly and unspectacularly into B and thence from B through to C and finally to E. The more such events occur, the more the border itself becomes gradual and blending and less sharp, thus making the passage of genes back and forth an increasingly easy process.

Decrease of isolation must have begun in this very modest way. The old, tenuous, and accidental channels of communication subsequently became broadened. This process was certainly abetted by the fact that in a number of places in the world and, quite independently, the growth of the idea and practice of communal living occurred. This change accompanied agricultural development which presented the possibility of a more sedentary existence, accompanied by an increase in population size of the unit from what we have called a "clan" to a rural village or, in some cases, to a metropolitan community.

At first, such communities could certainly remain in almost complete isolation from other such centers and retain within them isolations based on class structure, but as the unit becomes larger and more powerful it will begin to expand its activities in a centrifugal way. Forays of this sort would bring about increased contacts with neighboring groups, leading to the familiar round of misunderstandings, suspicions, fear, group hysteria, and war. These tragic diseases of the social system, however, have always had as a by-product a greatly increased gene exchange. Sexual contacts during and following such violent phases started the genetic breakdown of many isolates at a very early time, even before the historic period.

If given time, a few genes can go a long way. Thus an early and very minor amount of interbreeding can have effects that can be discerned thousands of years later. It is important to recognize that the kind of breakdown of isolation that is being discussed here does not depend on any process of mass intermarriage but, quite the opposite, significant changes usually occur by an almost undetectable genetic amalgamation which began before recorded history and has continued in recent centuries.

Up to this point we have dealt only with contacts between adjacent growing population units, individuals of which encountered one another at their distribution borders. As more efficient means of sea travel were developed, Grecian odysseys, Polynesian sea voyages, and Roman commercial and military travels made it possible for contacts to be established between the travelers and resident peoples in quite remote areas, people who were often quite distinct genetically as well as culturally.

Because efficient means of transportation must have behind it a relatively high degree of cultural advancement, voyaging peoples have always been technically more advanced than the peoples that they "discovered." It is not surprising that early voyagers almost completely misunderstood what they found. Isolation had so fostered cultural divergence that the basic genetic similarities between discoverer and discovered were not apparent behind the smoke screen of these superficial differences.

From the genetic point of view, the far-flung voyages and "exploration" of the world by European adventurers and their crews had considerable effect. The number of children produced among the people visited may have been relatively small but, throughout the world, these children were quite widely accepted and reared and there were few sedentary peoples who escaped at least a small incursion of European genes during this time. This type of gene flow, however, was largely a one-way process, that is, from the mobile into the nonmobile population. In other words, it was mostly due to sexual contacts which lacked permanence; only rarely did the voyager return with his native partner and children to Europe, a process which would have resulted in gene flow back in that direction. The final and perhaps the most important event for the understanding of the modern condition of human gene pools was the migration of large blocks of settlers, mostly from Europe and Great Britain, to almost every part of the globe. This was by far the most revolutionary genetic and cultural event in the history of mankind. With these migrations, almost all really effective isolation was broken down at least to some degree. Perhaps the least effect on genetic recombination was in those countries where the resident populations, following some violence, submitted to colonial rule. Although the violent phase probably resulted in some gene flow, the corps of colonial administrators which followed have tended to transplant segments of their own cultures and gene pools more or less unaltered to foreign shores.

The historical outcome has been almost universally the reduction of resisting native groups through war and disease to numerical inferiority. Bitter struggles of this kind in the Americas and Australia represented virtual replacements of the original gene pools of the geographical area by others, with relatively little gene flow from the aboriginal into the settler population.

The genetic recombination which took place between the different settler factions is much more important than that between settler and aboriginal. In the United States, for example, the present culture is an emergent one which tends to discourage the direct transplanting and rekindling of the details of ancestral culture. Under such relative freedom from cultural restraints, marriage between persons of diverse British Isles and European backgrounds has occurred so extensively and freely that any genetic integrity that these gene-pool subdivisions may have retained up to the period of migration was lost, except for a few artificially maintained enclaves. The same is true of Brazil, where, however, the aboriginal gene pools fared better than usual, amalgamating with both European and African elements.

This statement, of course, should not be taken to indicate that newly populous countries, like Brazil, the United States, and Australia, represent freely interbreeding gene pools. Large segments, because of religion or social custom have held tenaciously to the ancestral bonds of isolation. Some such groups remain to this day as cultural, social, and indeed genetic incarnations closely resembling the past. The major flow of history, however, has long since passed these by. The emergent cultures of the present century will slowly continue to engulf these formerly powerful influences.

The population explosion and the human gene pool today

Since the days of the maximum separation of man into local groups, two major changes have occurred. Both are of major genetic importance. First, there has been and continues to be a recombination of genes formerly held in strong isolates. Second, the breakdown of isolates has been accompanied by a colossal rise in the total size of the human population of the world from a few millions to thousands of millions.[1] We must attempt to understand the broad importance of each of these events.

Genetic recombination will have one major and all-pervading effect: it will promote genetic variability. Gene recombination even within an inbred group is probably a far more important source of genetic variability than new mutations. With the change-over from isolation to interbreeding in human populations, release of variability and the production of millions of unique combinations of human genes can occur and is occurring at an enormously increased rate. Both those who rejoice in hope for genetic betterment and those who fear genetic worsening are justified in their viewpoints. As the variability spreads both things will occur; there will be both more geniuses and more imbeciles. Genetic variability, furthermore, has a far better chance of being expressed in our large modern populations for the simple reason that far more recombinations can occur and more of them survive. Man is becoming more variable than less and the process has only just begun.

Although the genetic effects of large world populations cannot be set down as wholly bad, a soaring world population has nongenetic effects which are the rightful concern of everyone. World food resources are indeed eventually limited, even if technology were to permit us to double or even treble the present world supply. What nonbiologists do not seem to realize, however, is that the genetic material is absolutely unlimited in its innate capacity to reproduce. Environmental space, on the other hand, is strictly limited. Population size increases will have to be checked by rational action and the size of the population brought into a comfortable equilibrium with world food resources. If no rational action to control population is taken, inevitable checks, with accompanying starvation and human misery, will sooner or later slow down and stop population growth. In view of the difficulties now encountered in feeding people across the world, even with present technical advances, it is imperative that this equilibrium point be reached as soon as possible.

Economic theories which hold that continued growth rates must be maintained sooner or later will have to come to grips with the simple biological fact that the present growth of world population is only temporary; equilibration of birth and death rates is inevitable. In much the same way, the existence of religious tenets which forbid the limitation of human reproduction by simple mechanical or chemical means represents a tragic ignorance of the biological consequences. Human reproduction in all countries and for all peoples must be limited for the reason that living space is limited whereas the capacity of the genetic material is not. The hour which will permit willful and sensible controlled limitation is late.

Summary

Man comprises a single biological species because matings between persons of even the most diverse racial origins produce normal, healthy children which are themselves fertile. Gaps between species, on the other hand, are characterized by reproductive failure and are ordinarily unbridgeable. Racial gaps show no such fundamental genetic crossing disabilities. *Homo sapiens* was born in a small population and through many thousands of years prior to the historical period spread to all habitable parts of the globe. The major gene pool became subdivided into many thousands of local gene pools. Even at the height of isolation it is probable that occasional gene exchange took place at the borders of the clans, permitting a minor gene flow between groups to take place stepwise through many human populations. Both a long time and complete isolation are necessary conditions for species formation. Neither existed as the human races were formed. Following the attainment of social stability and village structure, contacts between geographically adjacent peoples were broadened and gene flow increased.

With the attainment by certain cultures of more efficient means of transportation, wide-ranging journeys brought together peoples who were dissimilar in superficial genetic characters and widely dissimilar in culture. Gene flow, mostly from the culturally more advanced into the culturally less advanced, was the inevitable result.

The most important source of mass genetic recombination has been among and between the European and African settler factions in the New World and among European stocks alone in Australia. By and large, the settlers in these areas have shed many of the cultural traditions that served to reinforce isolation. The result has been not only the emergence of new cultures which are truly modern in orientation and outlook but genepool breakdown and recombination on an unprecedented scale. In addition to recombination, there has been an enormous surge in population size. Whereas large size and genetic recombination alone are not intrinsically bad, the danger of outproducing the food supply poses grave problems for the species. If this is permitted to happen in the human case, it follows that great suffering will result. The only foreseeable escape from chaos is birth control.

Chapter 11

HEREDITY AND HUMAN UNDERSTANDING

Relative unimportance of group differences in heredity [1]

GENETIC differences between individuals frequently have large and important effects. As we have seen, intellectual endowment, physical coordination, or the ability to resist disease may show great genetic variation even between individuals who come from the same family. No differences like these, however, characterize groups. Those which do are superficial characters like skin color and hair structure. Differences between human groups in language and customs are vast, but these differences are culturally determined; they have no genetic ingredient at all.

To be blunt, there is no scientific evidence that forces one to the view that any group is genetically superior or inferior to any other group. This is true unless one is prepared to argue that superiority must rest on superficial characters or wishes to single out as inferior certain very small human populations which may carry a high frequency of one or more disease-producing genes. On the whole, however, the statement is valid and those who do not understand why are confusing cultural inheritance with biological inheritance. Cultural inheritance has become so powerful a force for shaping a man and his group that it transcends biological inheritance in importance. The existence of this powerful environmental influence, of course, increases the scientific difficulties of obtaining evidence on possible group genetic differences. The existence of individual variation makes it even harder. Yet, despite these difficulties, our testing methods are good enough to reveal important differences if they do, in fact, exist. Such differences have not been found.

The historic isolation of human groups gave each a different set of experiences and values; languages and cultures have thus become different. Yet the extraordinary unity of underlying needs and desires of all people has resulted in a rather small number of basic ends: these are the threads that unite all cultures. There are almost as many ways to try to achieve security for one's family as there are cultures. Even though the means are not always comprehensible across cultures, the ends are.

If there is no strong genetic ingredient in most cultural differences, then why should the matter be brought up in a discussion frankly concerned with the importance of biological inheritance? The answer lies in the simple fact that confusion over the evaluation of nature and nurture is the greatest source of misunderstanding among peoples. The biological facts provide a basis for dispelling this confusion.

Some persons find it easy to mislead themselves into believing that things like cannibalism, shoe-making, or facility with a particular language have strong bases in biological inheritance. At the moment of birth, the son of a shoemaker is free enough. His genes determine him no more to be a shoemaker than a farmer or a mathematician. But certain cultures begin immediately to weld their youth with strong ties to the culture. Personal, psychological, and frequently manual skills are molded in the direction of specific activities.

Every brain, however, has a slightly different genetic background and for this reason not every brain is equally capable of being molded by the dictates of the culture. Genetic variation provides, of course, a minority of really unteachable persons, those who have some basic mental defect. There appear also to be categories of minds having inborn inflexibilities of less severity. Such conditions may predispose their carriers to various types of asocial or antisocial behavior. All human groups have a share of such minorities. Their existence is not necessarily a bad thing because it is from their ranks that constructive rebellion can arise. All cultures transfer a certain number of preposterous and senseless customs along with their more positive achievements. If each human mind were identical and fully malleable, we might indeed find groups which as a whole could be called saintly or sinful. In truth, however, variability assures us of the continuation of the present confusing and unwieldly mixture within each culture, with little agreement between cultures of the definition of a saint or a sinner.

A fallacy—judging brains from cultures

We are often tempted to judge the inborn mental capacities of a group of people by the monuments of art and science that have been produced by them. There are several *non sequiturs* in such a procedure. The first and most glaring one is that art and to a very great degree science as well are achievements of individuals, not of groups. If art and science are to prosper, the society must permit it. The function of the group in these endeavors is not to perform but to condone, to create conditions and to encourage the free expression of the individual. It is only under these conditions that the exceptional gene combinations producing a brain capable of being guided into these great human achievements may express itself. To think that the amazing brain of a Leonardo da Vinci would be self-determining, like skin color, in any cultural context is to misunderstand the whole relationship between heredity and environment with respect to traits of human behavior. The genes of the great masters of

Renaissance Italy are still there today among their descendants, albeit in new and unique combinations. If the achievements of the past are not being matched in the present it is not the fault of the genes, even though the exceptional combinations are always rare. The fault lies rather with the grinding poverty, the aftermath of war, the subtle effects of political unrest and upheaval that destroy in whole or in part the opportunity of individual expression.

Renaissances are rare indeed in history and their lives have been short. Influences which permit individual freedom of expression without misuse are difficult to achieve. They tend to suffer quick political repression. Each renaissance has characteristics of its own. Much has been made, for example, of the current flowering of science in the modern world; scientists have suddenly become a much larger component in many societies. Scientific endeavor has been recognized by cultures in all parts of the world as indispensible to the welfare of modern society.

A striking example of the sudden flowering of both art and science when conditions promoting them crystallize is represented by the ancient civilizations of Mexico and Peru. Along with these extraordinary cultures there existed simultaneously, in very closely adjacent geographical areas, groups of American Indians which retained Stone Age cultures no more advanced artistically or scientifically than those of the present-day Stone Age groups in Australia or Africa.

In the Middle American case, it is very clear that the peoples who developed these cultures and those who did not were genetically very similar. All had been derived only a short time before from sparse migrations into America across the land-bridge over Bering Strait. This is not to say that there is not some genetic difference between the different tribes of American Indians. They do, as mentioned previously, show some stature and minor physical differences related to the tendencies, already discussed, which occur in small populations. But aside from these very minor differences, American Indians, as their blood-group frequencies also bear out, are closely similar genetically and this would include their basic mental capacities as well.

The Mayas of Yucatan, with their agriculture, art, calendar mathematics, and to some degree social organization, were one of the wonders of the ancient world. Nevertheless, there is no reason to believe that they, as a group, were genetically superior to any other American tribes. Not far away from them, in Guatemala, Costa Rica, and Panama dwelt tribes whose economies continued to be based on food-gathering and in some cases, like the Chocós of Panama, have essentially retained this culture to the present day. Like many of the ancient civilizations of the Middle East, Greece, Egypt, and Ur these Middle American civilizations succumbed to diverse pressures of internal and external forces. Yet in many cases the genes live on, sometimes even on the same sites. One illustration is the pitifully undernourished and vestigial tribe of Yucatan that still lives around the crumbling temples of the past.

If art, science, and urban civilization were taken as a measure of basic intelligence, archaeological science would tell us that the genetic basis of intelligence 3,000 years ago was absent from the British Isles and northern Europe, where there were mostly primitive warring bands. It would tell us that intelligence was present only in spotty fashion around the world, in Middle America, in Egypt, and in China. We would further have to conclude that in this short time the genetic capacity for advanced culture suddenly appeared in some groups, disappeared in others, and remained unchanged in still others. We arrive at an absurdity; genetic change could not occur that fast in a slow breeder like man, even if the most extraordinarily unlikely kinds of selective pressures were applied.

A person raised in our modern technological society may find it difficult to accept the possibility that a person from one of the few surviving Stone Age cultures may have basic intellectual equipment similar to his own. An individual reared in a Stone Age culture and suddenly removed from it does indeed have difficulty in learning to do what appear to be simple tasks, despite what is usually interpreted as a "willingness" to learn. Performance like this is often thought to be due to some sort of mental defectiveness, even by those well-disposed towards "native" peoples.

Without probing into the obvious area of the kinds of psychological motivation which will persuade one man that he should do another's bidding, it may be noted that communication between cultures is more difficult than it seems. Language is a key cultural trait and some languages are very poor in words and conceptualizations. In most complex cultures we proliferate our vocabularies and come to depend on verbalization to an extraordinarily high degree. A person who is not reared in such a culture, but whose language is more limited, suffers a severe communication handicap. The result is a kind of cultural mental defectiveness based on the lack of a rich language.

Such mental defectiveness might be likened to that which is associated with deafness from birth as it occurs in advanced cultures. Except under the most rigorous training, and not always then, the deaf person is cut off from communication. He is forced into a defectiveness of mind which becomes in our culture a severe mental handicap. Like his Stone Age counterpart, whose performance may resemble word deafness rather than sensory deafness, this handicap may be unrelated to his basic genetic mental equipment. It is the direct outcome of an imperfect means of communication.

Communication among primitive peoples is by no means as verbalized as those of other cultures, nor does it involve the simple pantomimic procedure which seems, to our culture, the only adequate substitute for speech. Symbols, labels, emotional states, dance movements, or use of art objects and ceremony form means of communication among primitive peoples which are only vaguely understood by advanced cultures. Indeed, the shoe may sometimes be on the other foot; relative mental defectiveness in the sense of a disability to comprehend and communicate on a certain mental and especially emotional level may lie with the overintellectualized product of a verbalized culture.

The accomplishments of art, science, engineering, and urbanity are not the only monuments to human creativity. High moral and ethical sense are equally monumental and all groups have cultivated them to some degree. It is a paradoxical and humbling thought for the adherent of Western civilization when he contemplates the fact that persons from his culture have frequently so misused their power. Technically less advanced peoples around the world have been subjected to repeated frightful repressions, to say nothing of the less overt, subtle indignities that strike so deeply into the human mind.

Civilization does not consist only of the modern veneer; it must also include capacity for intelligent cooperation, solution of common problems in a peaceful manner, and provision for essential and enlightened training of the young. The antisocial element must be intelligently regulated and means must be found for generating responsible leadership. Both technically advanced and technically retarded civilizations have groped over the centuries for ways of solving these problems, that is, for the development of civilization in its truest sense. The technically advanced societies have made almost no attempts to understand the ethical codes and social structures that their power found so easy to subvert. Without overvaluing or sentimentalizing nontechnical societies, we may point out that the result has been a wastage of human heritage and a destruction of possible philosophical contributions to the solution of the problems that face mankind.

The matter is pertinent to the present discussion because the arrogance of Western civilization has for centuries claimed justification for its values on the basis that its proponents were somehow superior, in a genetic sense, to other peoples. This idea has been less overtly stated in the present century but still exists in a strong covert form. The science of heredity has been evoked, as by Hitler, as producing evidence that this is so. Let us state categorically that the science of heredity provides no evidence for the truth of this idea.

The conclusion of the foregoing discussion is that genetic differences between human groups in brain capacity, that is, in basic human behavior, are insignificant, if they exist at all.[2] Again, it should be emphasized that this appears to be true for groups only. There are far-reaching genetic differences in brain capacity between individual persons. The only way we can understand our fellow man is to approach him as an individual, reaching for an understanding of the basic similarities between ourself and him—similarities which may be so externally encrusted with cultural differences as to require great intelligence and skill to locate. Locating them, however, is one of the truly inspirational events of life for the humanist.

Genetic improvement of the human species

Knowledge of genetic principles should enable us to improve the genetic condition of our species. About 2 percent of live births carry some harmful hereditary defect of sense organs, skeleton, blood, or brain. Corrective measures of a medical sort are possible in many cases, but the majority of these unfortunate individuals must not only carry a heavy personal handicap through life but are frequently a burden on their families and society. What can be done about this? Can society practice some sort of selection process like that described in Chapter 8 and eliminate or greatly reduce these conditions? Unfortunately, the answer is that we can reduce them only slightly.

During the early days of genetics, optimism on this subject ran high. Application of genetic principles to the improvement of the human species has been called eugenics. There are two general approaches. The first may be called preventive eugenics; it emphasizes the need for measures designed to decrease the frequency of serious hereditary defects. Progressive eugenics, on the other hand, concerns itself not so much with the elimination of the obviously bad but with the encouragement of what is judged to be good heredity.[3]

Prevention of the birth of a defective individual is a principle that meets with wide approval, yet is in practice difficult to achieve. Quite obviously, a person who is himself seriously handicapped with a hereditary condition should be discouraged from reproducing, thus accomplishing some selection against the gene concerned. Indeed, laws exist which provide for sterilization in certain cases. As almost all hereditary defects of importance are recessive to the normal condition, however, selection against the gene by preventing reproduction of those having it in double dose is not very efficient in a population sense. This is because the great number of people who are normal yet carry it are most important as a source of perpetuation and recognition of these carriers in many cases is not possible. Study of family histories, however, may enable a genetic counselor in some cases to estimate the probability that a defective child will be produced. Nevertheless, the laws of chance, genetic recombination, and recessiveness being what they are, accurate estimation of probability in most cases is not possible in our present state of knowledge.

The fact that many hereditary conditions are not based on the major effect of just one gene pair helps to reduce our ability to predict. Often, a number of gene pairs, each with individually small effect, form the hereditary basis of the character. This "many genes with small effects" type of inheritance makes accurate predictions in such cases virtually impossible. On top of this are the effects of the environment, which also vary from character to character. Mental characters, the ones that interest us the most, are especially affected by both of these analytically difficult and blurring influences.

For all of these reasons, preventive eugenics, operating through sterilization laws or through genetic counseling, has not so far been very effective in bringing about large-scale betterment of human gene pools. Despite this pessimistic appraisal of the population effects, however, it is well to remember that every defective individual that can be avoided represents a positive gain. Genetic counseling should be expanded and full use made of present knowledge. Just as any measure which will prevent even a minute increase in the mutation rate by radiations or chemicals in the modern age is a positive step, so is any measure which reduces the frequency of harmful genes, even if it does so only slightly.

Progressive eugenics consists of encouraging those with "good" genes to have a lot of children, thereby enabling these persons to contribute a greater share of genes to future generations than those whose genes are not so "good." The argument most frequently advanced is that we must breed from our best brains so as to prevent deterioration of human mental capacity. Proponents of progressive eugenics point with alarm to the very clear fact that groups in the lower socio-economic and educational levels frequently have the highest birth rates. Thus, population-wise, the genes carried by them are being favored by selection.

There is no question that some groups perform better than others in science, art, and business but whether this is due to a higher concentration of genes leading to superior brains is highly questionable, as this writer has pointed out before. The evidence that is sometimes cited to support the idea is very weak. Yet this is such a difficult matter on which to get incontrovertible evidence that it should be pointed out that slight genetic differences might exist between some groups. We just do not know for sure. On the other hand, if such differences exist they are certainly far too small to warrant the kind of social action frequently advocated by progressive eugenicists.

In conclusion, let us recommend preventive eugenics but proceed very cautiously in progressive eugenics. A firm scientific basis for the latter does not now exist. It is unrealistic to be overly preoccupied with the possibility of slight biological superiorities based on the hereditary material.

Inbreeding and outbreeding in humans: is either tendency biologically desirable?

When marriage occurs between two persons who come from precisely the same minor gene-pool subdivision, this represents a marriage between closely related persons. When a population group has a large number of such marriages, it may be said to be inbred. When inbreeding is very close, that is, between brother and sister or between first cousins, the probability of genetic impairment of offspring increases. This comes about through the possibility that one or more deleterious recessive genes, carried in hidden single dose in the two parents, may by chance be passed on to the child from both parents. This will happen with a higher degree of probability the more closely related two individuals are.

Inbreeding, however, is not intrinsically bad. For example, if a brother-sister marriage were to involve two persons who by some extremely remote chance carried no damaging genes at all, there would be no bad biological effects whatever. Nevertheless, the frequency of harmful recessive genes is high in all human groups which have been studied. This makes close inbreeding quite risky and it is for this reason that it is advisable to avoid it if possible. The risk declines as the two marriage partners are less closely related.

The opposite of inbreeding is outbreeding, that is, the condition that we recognize in a population wherein most of the marriages are between persons who are only distantly related. Just as brother-sister mating represents the closest possible type of inbreeding, so marriage between two individuals of widely separate geographical (racial) origin, from New Guinea and northern Europe, for example, would represent the widest type of outbreeding.

Unlike inbreeding, there is no genetic reason why outbreeding should be undesirable. As far as damaging recessive genes are concerned, these would be expected to be covered up in the offspring of an outcross, reducing the chance of an affected child. This effect, however, results from even a moderate outcross within most minor gene pools. Outbreeding produces a certain amount of "hybrid vigor" but, again, this effect is not more pronounced in wide (interracial) outcrosses than it is in moderate outcrosses.

From its very inception, the populations of our species have been relatively closely inbred in small isolated populations. We have seen that this process promoted divergence between groups and tended towards uniformity within the group, although the latter never proceeded very far. In the last 5,000 years there has been an increase of outbreeding generally as the isolations have broken down, but almost all modern continental populations have complex mixtures of inbreeding and outbreeding.

By and large, Brazil serves as the best example in the modern world of a large (50 million) population where the original genetic racial markers have been to a considerable extent lost through recombination. Ancestrally, these genes were derived from European (Portugal), African, and American Indian sources. In the initial settling of the country, recombination and outcrossing were the rule. As the towns in the interior were settled, however, a new cycle of inbreeding ensued among the descendants of the original outcrosses. These new isolates, together with a small number of groups which were isolated from the beginning and remained so, contribute to the complexity of the breeding system. Nevertheless, the Brazilian population cannot be correctly referred to as a multiracial society, a term which would imply the separate coexistence in the same geographical area of migrant groups of separate racial (continental) origin. Perhaps the best term to apply to the Brazilian situation would be "recombinational population." Except for the very small number of original enclaves, both the genes of the people and, indeed, their ancient cultural influences have undergone reassortment into new patterns.

In the sense that the term has been used above, the population of the United States may also be regarded as recombinational, although the bulk of the recombination involves genes from most of the European countries. There is a lesser, but certainly not insignificant, amount of recombination involving genes from Africa and Asia as well.

In countries such as modern Europe, the United States, Brazil, and other American countries, the term "race" has very limited use. In the strict scientific sense, as we have seen earlier, race refers to a genetically recognizable gene pool which originated in a specific geographic position within the species as a whole. Before the major world migrations of the modern era, it would have been a relatively easy matter to assign any one individual to one of the major geographic races, although the drawing of exact lines between them was never possible because of blending at the borders. Migration from the original continent and intermarriage between persons from different original geographical isolates has destroyed, over whole continents, any analytical validity or descriptive scientific usefulness of the concept of race. Application of the term becomes meaningless except perhaps for those groups of people who have remained in isolation at the ancestral site or since leaving it.

Which is best, from the point of view of the genetic health of future generations, inbreeding, outbreeding, or some combination of the two? From the population point of view, it is the writer's opinion that it does not make any difference what the pattern is, as long as the inbreeding is no closer than marriage of second cousins. Outbreeding is always connected with some degree of "hybrid vigor" but this vigor is not so pronounced in the human case as to make it worthwhile cultivating. Furthermore, recombination begins to break down hybrid vigor a few generations after an interracial cross (or wide cross within a race), so that in a population sense this vigor cannot be retained for very long under normal human breeding systems. Recombination itself does not lead to new gene combinations which are, on the whole, biologically either more or less desirable. Thus, new combinations of nose and ear shape, blood groups, and skin colors would follow outcrossing, but there is no evidence that any significant proportion of these would be either advantageous or disadvantageous.

The same is true with regard to mental traits. As there appears to be no significant concentration of genetically based mental superiority in any group in the first place, there need be no concern that such traits would be eroded by outcrossing. On the contrary, under outcrossing, the range of variability would increase, thus increasing the chance of realizing an occasional gene recombination leading to exceptional brilliance as well as the reverse. As in other traits, these occasional extremes would be expected, but the great bulk of genotypes would be hardly discernibly different from currently existing arrays.

Role of human differences in human divisiveness

Populations of the human species first became subdivided into geographical races. Major geographical isolates were followed by greater and greater subdivision into sub-races, clans, and local tribes of every conceivable kind. As these divisions arose, communication between them was suppressed. As we have seen, most geographical isolates of man have some small degree of genetic difference but it is the cultural differences that become really important.

Human clannishness does not hold to simple geographical lines. Even in small villages or developing urban communities, clannishness is characteristic, with resultant class formation. Although different classes of a society, which become gene pools within gene pools, may have originated in some geographical way, geography is not needed for human custom to perpetuate them. Prince and pauper, aristocrat and serf, noble and untouchable are basically artificial subdivisions made wholly according to haphazard human whims, not on biological grounds.

What forces or drives our species to band together in tight little groups of narrow outlook? One may only speculate on the answer at the present time and hope that research on social behavior will soon provide us with a definitive rational answer. The answer must lie in the practical fulfillment of some basic psychological need for security in the face of the uncertainties, complexities, and difficulties of life. By adopting the attitudes and values of a small group, we avoid the agonizing process of learning through our own individual experience to cope with the variables of our social environment. Thus it is easier to adopt the major viewpoints of the group, unquestioned and ready-made, as we must of necessity adopt unquestioningly so many other minor things which are taught to us as part of our culture.

This brings us to the attitude of one clan towards another clan. The lack of meaningful communication over the generations between the splinter groups of man has been a divisive force of gigantic proportions, and has set the stage continually for the major social disease, war. Prior to the development of modern communications, knowledge of cultures other than the one into which we were born was almost nonexistent. At best, information rested on the highly individually colored accounts of a few "voyagers" who went across to the other side of the tracks, made observations and returned with "the truth." Half-truth is what they really returned with, and that is often more dangerous than sheer uninformed prejudice.

In these days when communication is easier and when individuals are able to make independent judgments of cultures other than the ones they were reared in, perhaps the most dangerous new element is the facile generalization based on wholly inadequate evidence. Learning to make independent observations is laudable, but drawing valid conclusions about heredity and environment from a small number of observations is virtually impossible and yet is a trap that snares almost everyone.

Generalizations in this field are difficult because of the number of variables that must be taken into account. The greater the number of variables, the tougher becomes the evaluation of cause and effect without an increasingly larger and larger sample size. If the variables are few, the amateur is often successful. Many persons, for example, who are not necessarily accomplished meteorologists, are nonetheless very good weather experts. Repeated daily observations of a relatively small number of variables, actually about three, wind direction, cloud form, and barometric pressures, soon enable a perceptive person to make quite reasonable diagnoses of conditions and, consequently, weather predictions of some value.

Characterizing human beings, however, is another matter. Each person is unlike any other person, past, present, or future in genotype. Second, his life experience, which shaped his personality, has also been unique. Accordingly, behavior of an individual, whether godlike or criminal, will not necessarily allow us to predict how the next individual will act.

If we cannot predict how the individual will act, it is an even harder job to form judgments of groups. Yet, traditionally, our cultures have handed us stereotypes as to what English or French or Japanese or Italians are supposed to be like. As a conversational commonplace, we glibly employ the concept of "type," as if men could be typed like wind direction or carpet tacks. Even if we do not accept the stereotypes which our various cultures apply, our own personal observations of individual cases, much as we would wish to be scientific about it, cannot help very much. For example, we may encounter an Italian (apologies, please!) who is kind but rather secretive, comes from Milan, has blonde hair and large feet and who stammers. He wears glasses, is interested in politics, runs an insurance business, enjoys opera, and so on. From these observations, and even from hundreds like them, it is almost impossible to draw any but the most cautious generalizations about Italians, if indeed such generalizations would have any real utility in any event.

This brings us to the crux of this section. Broad generalizations about people, especially as regards the characteristics of the groups from which they come, are almost sure to be wrong for some members of the group. What valid stereotypes we are able to erect, furthermore, are due to the influence of culture. There are no genetic stereotypes. Each individual has his own unique genotype, and the way this genotype will interact with the culture in which he is reared will display individuality.

Divisiveness among men has been and continues to be the greatest tragedy of the human condition. The psychological fears nourished by ignorance and isolation lead to the formation of cultural cliques, which have been referred to as "in-groups." Another group, not conforming or belonging, may represent, relative to the first, an "out-group." [4] When a real or fancied danger threatens or appears to threaten an individual or his in-group, a common redress is the designation of an out-group as scapegoat. A large measure of intergroup hatreds thus result rather simply from the psychology of fear. Fear both originates and feeds on ignorance and prejudice. Overt acts may produce reactions leading to the accentuation of fear and so the cycle continues.

So-called racial tensions are thus mostly externalized fears. These fears have no rational basis in biology. The slight racial differences between men (skin color, for example) are significant only as convenient labels by which a fancied out-group member can be quickly identified. By the use of such labels, discrimination becomes simpler. When the biological label is lacking, the individual belonging to the scapegoat minority has frequently been forced to label himself, as the untouchables in India or the Jews under the Nazis in Germany were forced to do.

Intergroup tensions probably cannot be much lessened by simply knowing their cause. When a certain emotional state is reached, simple knowledge is not enough. The most hopeful course seems to be the lessening of the initial fears themselves, rather than any attempt to provide a remedy after the situation has gained emotional strength.

In our day, fear of wild beasts, storms, and disease have largely given way to fear of one's fellow man and the threat that he may pose to one's financial security. Knowledge of the simple biology of man, as outlined in this book, may serve to lessen these fears, to direct them away from the absurdities that enter into the emotional state when fears are externalized and fastened onto others.

Summary

Although individual genetic differences are frequently large, genetic differences between groups appear to be small. There is no evidence that basic mental differences did in fact accumulate during the isolation-inbreeding phase of human development. In general, wide differences in individual mental performance within a culture are likely to have a strong genetic component, whereas differences between groups are likely to be strongly determined by the environmental influences of the culture itself. The conclusion is drawn that the chasms of behavior and mental differences between various groups of *Homo sapiens* are principally cultural and thus biologically superficial. The genetic component in physical differences is large, but the differences themselves are small, chiefly involving body build and pigmentations.

Isolation, until recent centuries, was profound. It led not only to genetic divergence but also to profound cultural differences. Noncommunication led to extreme divisiveness, mutual misunderstandings, suspicions, and fears. Fear leads to consolidation of an in-group and the external expression of these fears comes out as prejudice. As fears of the physical world have been largely removed by scientific understanding and control, fear of one's fellow man has become more prominent. Minor genetic differences between groups become magnified because they serve as convenient labels.

Destruction of barriers between men will call for the leveling of cultural differences and the forging of an emergent world culture. Because human ends are universally the same, this should be a realizable goal. As cultural barriers are removed, increased intermarriage between persons of different genetic background may be expected to increase, although breakdown of cultural divergences does not depend on such intermarriage. The biology of man and the study of human heredity provides no evidence that this result would be undesirable in any way as far as human biology is concerned. Contrariwise, a considerable degree of inbreeding may occur without genetic deterioration of the population as a whole, although very close inbreeding is risky.

NOTES

All scientific discovery has a strong social element. The individual who finally strikes the touchstone and articulates disjointed facts is able to do so only because he is standing on a foundation of facts that has been built by others before him. As in the solution of a jigsaw puzzle, the scientist credited later with a discovery may often have actually added only one small piece to the puzzle himself. This piece may in fact have been crucial and suddenly provides a glimpse of the larger picture for the first time. Very often, too, the most important first function of the discoverer is to take apart puzzle pieces which have been forced together into wrong and confusing patterns by his overzealous predecessors.

In a book like this, the fruits of the labors of hundreds or even thousands of investigators extending often over a century or more may be summarily compressed into a single sentence. Little real justice can be done to the work of these investigators short of exhaustive technical treatises, which of course exist on almost all of these subjects. Yet the reader of a general book on a scientific subject is entitled to something more than the bald statements of the summarizer. For the annotation of the chapters, therefore, I have attempted here and there to mention a few original scientific works which were somehow pivotal in the discovery process. My only regret in using this method is that it may cause the reader to be oblivious of the enormous expenditure of human effort that it took to set the stage for every discovery.

1. Origin of the Individual

1. The notion that life could be spontaneously generated and lacked any historical continuity with the past delayed progress in this field incalculably. The end of this idea came at an evening lecture by Louis

Pasteur in 1864. Pasteur demonstrated to his audience ingeniously contrived bottles of rich culture medium which had remained sterile because contamination with microorganisms from the air had been prevented. With characteristic flair he said: "And, therefore, gentlemen, I could point to that liquid and say to you, I have taken my drop of water from the immensity of creation, and I have taken it full of the elements appropriate to the development of inferior beings. And I wait, I watch, I question it, begging it to recommence for me the beautiful spectacle of the first creation. But it is dumb, dumb since these experiments were begun several years ago; it is dumb because I have kept it from the only thing that man cannot produce, from the germs which float in the air, from Life, for Life is a germ and a germ is Life. Never will the doctrine of spontaneous generation recover from the mortal blow of this simple experiment." (R. Vallery-Radot, *The Life of Pasteur*, Westminster, A. Constable and Company, Ltd., 1902.)

2. The most striking recent experiments are those of Stanley Miller. He took a mixture of simple organic compounds and subjected them to the high-energy conditions of a series of electric shocks, simulating conditions that might have existed during pre-life eras on the earth. Within this mixture there were artificially produced a number of amino acids, that is, proteins of the simplest sort. Amino acids serve as the main building blocks from which, under the guidance of the hereditary information, the cells of modern organisms build their unique complexities. (Stanley L. Miller, "A production of amino acids under possible primitive earth conditions," *Science*, 117 [1953], 528–29.)

3. If proper stimulation is applied, some eggs will begin development without being fertilized. Pincus, for example, has been able to rear fatherless rabbits from unfertilized eggs, although the number of cases was small. (G. Pincus, "The breeding of some rabbits produced by recipients of artificially activated ova," *Proc. Natl. Acad. Sci. U.S.*, 25 [1939], 557–59.)

4. It was the German anatomist Oscar Hertwig who, in 1875, made the key discovery of the fusion of the nuclei. The clarity with which he recognized this point dispelled centuries of confusion and uncertainty about heredity.

2. The Hereditary Information

1. The apathy and disregard with which fundamental scientific dis-

coveries are often met is nowhere clearer than in the case of Mendel's work. An obscure Austrian monk, Mendel worked alone in his monastery garden. From his breeding experiments, mostly with pea plants, he perceived with great clarity the basic principles of inheritance, common to all living things. His use of single characters, test crosses, quantitative methods, and study of ratios were not understood by contemporary biologists. They ignored rather than tried to understand them. Although his classic paper was published in 1865, it lay virtually unnoticed until about 1900, when this extraordinary piece of work was "discovered."

2. A fertilized egg, or the individual which develops from it, may sometimes, as indicated here, have both genes of a pair identical to one another. Such individuals, illustrated by the WW and ww guinea pigs, are referred to as *homozygous*. Carrier individuals, having one dominant and one recessive gene, such as the Ww guinea pigs in this example, are referred to as *heterozygous*.

3. A simple model helps to illustrate principles here. Obtain two pairs of poker chips (two red and two blue) or two pairs of coins of different denomination. Taking the two blue chips, write W on one and w on the other, marking them only on one side. Do the same with two red chips. Using Fig. 6 as a guide, place the two blue chips face down on the table to represent the female's genotype. The male is to be represented by the two red chips. To model the formation of an egg by the female, shuffle the two blue chips, then move one of the two, at random, toward you to represent the female contribution to the as yet unfertilized egg. Shuffle the two red chips and draw one to represent the sperm. This one blue (from female) and one red (from male) are then combined to form the fertilized egg. On turning the chips over, one may see that you will have one of the four combinations illustrated in Fig. 6. In order to observe that a ratio of 1 WW to 2 WW to 1 ww will be obtained, it is best to model the raising of a family of a hundred offspring. This can be done by making a hundred such drawings and fertilizations with the chips and recording the results of each on a separate sheet of paper. After each drawing, the chips used should be used again to model the genotypes of the two parents and should be throughly reshuffled before drawing again, assuring that chance only is involved in the selection of which of the two is to go into the egg or sperm.

4. To model sex chromosome behavior with poker chips, label both

the blue chips with X (the female condition). Two red chips are marked X and Y, respectively, to represent the male condition. Every egg produced will have an X, whereas half of the sperm will be Y and half X, resulting in half sons (XY) and half daughters (XX).

5. Two brilliant experiments provide the strongest kind of evidence that DNA is the hereditary material. The bacterium that causes pneumonia, *Pneumococcus,* comes with either a capsule around it (called S, for smooth) or without a capsule (called R, rough, because of the appearance of the outside edge of the cell). These are permanent hereditary types. Avery and his co-workers treated cultures of R cells with chemically purified DNA made from S cultures. Some R cells took up this DNA and were transformed into cells having the S character permanently, passing it on to their descendants. (O. T. Avery, C. M. MacLeod, and M. McCarty, "Studies on the chemical nature of the substance inducing transformation of Pneumococcal types," *J. Exptl. Med.,* 79 [1944], 137–58.)

A second experiment that also points to DNA as the crucial material in inheritance was done with a virus which parasitizes bacteria. The virus normally enters a bacterial cell and reproduces its kind inside. The virus particles are composed of protein and DNA. Hershey and Chase labeled the protein of an infective virus with radioactive sulphur and found that virtually none goes into the bacterium along with the virus infection. The hereditary information, it was concluded, resides in the DNA. (A. D. Hershey and M. Chase, "Independent functions of viral protein and nucleic acid in growth of bacteriophage," *J. Gen. Physiol.,* 36 [1952], 39–56.)

6. The so-called Watson-Crick model was proposed in a brilliant paper of only one page in 1953. Its significance lies in the simultaneously clarifying and galvanizing effects the hypothesis had throughout biochemistry. Not only were confusing facts suddenly understandable in the light of it, but great new areas of research were opened up, with the end as yet nowhere in sight. The authors received the Nobel Prize in Medicine in 1962. (J. D. Watson and F. H. C. Crick, "A structure for desoxyribose nucleic acid," *Nature,* 171 [1953], 737–38.)

7. For this extraordinary feat, the young biochemist Arthur Kornberg was awarded a Nobel Prize in 1959. In syntheses made so far, a small amount of intact DNA has been found necessary to "prime" the reaction. (A. Kornberg, "The biologic synthesis of deoxyribonucleic acid," *Science,* 131 [1960], 1503–8.)

3. Stability of the Hereditary Material

1. Similar mutants having dwarfing effects are known in a number of animals. In sheep, for example, it has been possible to trace the origin of short-legged or "ancon" sheep to two separate instances of mutation. One of these occurred in New England in 1791 and another in Norway in 1925. In both cases the discoverers built up flocks of animals descended from the original mutants. Like many of the mutants among domestic animals, the short-legged condition was useful. The new gene had no bad side effects on wool, meat, or general stamina but the fact that the short-legged sheep could not jump very well made fencing of them cheaper and easier than the normal varieties.

2. This fundamental discovery, one of the most important in this century, was made by H. J. Muller in 1927 and was work for which he received a Nobel Prize. It was no chance discovery. Muller had spent previous years working out ingenious, special genetic methods with fruit flies which would enable precise measurement of mutability. He prepared special "tester" chromosomes which were synthesized using genetic methods analogous to those of a chemist. His short paper ushered in a new epoch in genetic research. (H. J. Muller, "Artificial transmutation of the gene," *Science*, 66 [1927], 84–87.)

4. Combinations and Recombinations of Genes

1. Near the end of a brief paper on grasshopper chromosomes, published in December, 1902, Walter Sutton dropped the following remark: "I may finally call attention to the probability that the association of paternal and maternal chromosomes in pairs and their subsequent separation during the reducing division as indicated above may constitute the physical basis of the Mendelian law of heredity." This sentence marked the birth of the chromosome theory of heredity.

6. The Individual and His Group

1. Whereas it was Mendel who first introduced mathematical methods into the interpretations of results of individual crosses, the mathematics of gene pools came later. G. H. Hardy and W. Weinberg simultaneously pointed out that the binomial square law applies to the

formation of genotypes in sexual populations. Thus was founded the science of population genetics. (G. H. Hardy, "Mendelian proportions in a mixed population," *Science*, 28 [1908], 49–50.)

From this modest beginning, population genetics has seen the elaboration of a comprehensive theory of evolution based on descent with change in the gene composition of natural populations. The principal formulators of this theory and their key publications are: R. A. Fisher, *The Genetical Theory of Natural Selection*, Oxford, Clarendon Press, 1930; J. B. S. Haldane, *The Causes of Evolution*, New York, Harper and Brothers, 1932; S. Wright, "The roles of mutation, inbreeding, crossbreeding and selection in evolution," *Proc. Inter. Congr. Genet.*, 6th Congr., 1 [1932], 356–66.

7. Origin of the Human Species

1. These finds, as well as those of *Proconsul*, were made by L. S. B. Leakey. *Zinjanthropus* was described in a historic short paper. (L. S. B. Leakey, "A new fossil skull from Olduvai," *Nature*, 184 [1959], 491–93.) There have been many colorful and dedicated workers in the field of primate paleontology; unfortunately, only a few can be mentioned in the summary treatment given in this book. For details, see the book by Howells, listed in the General References.

2. The key workers on South African australopithecines were Robert Broom and Raymond Dart. The latter was first to publish a description. (R. Dart, "*Australopithecus africanus:* The man-ape of South Africa," *Nature*, 115 [1925], 195–99.) However, Broom began in 1936 a long series of discoveries at Sterkfontein. For some years, the significance of these discoveries for human evolution was not fully realized.

8. Evolutionary Forces as Applied to Man

1. The subject of evolutionary rates and their interpretation has grown into the most important new direction that paleontology has taken in this century. The leader in this field has been G. G. Simpson, several of whose books are: *The Meaning of Evolution*, New Haven, Yale University Press, 1949, and *The Major Features of Evolution*, New York, Columbia University Press, 1953.

2. This very clear example, on which the most recent work has been done by Kettlewell, is the only one of hundreds of well-known cases

of evolution in action. For accounts of this work see: Th. Dobzhansky, *Genetics and the Origin of Species*, New York, Columbia University Press, 1951; J. Huxley, *Evolution, The Modern Synthesis*, New York, Harper and Brothers, 1943; P. M. Sheppard, *Natural Selection and Heredity*, London, Hutchinson and Company, Ltd., 1958; G. L. Stebbins, Jr., *Variation and Evolution in Plants*, New York, Columbia University Press, 1950.

3. It has been above all Sewall Wright who has pioneered these calculations and who has brought home forcibly the importance of the "small population" effect.

10. The Historic Breakdown of Isolation

1. For a recent account of the facts of world population growth, see H. F. Dorn, "World population growth: an international dilemma," *Science*, 135 [1962], 283–90.

11. Heredity and Human Understanding

1. This chapter contains a number of judgments and conclusions of the writer. He is solely responsible for them.

2. Reprinted below is a statement issued by a UNESCO committee in 1951:

Statement on the Nature of Race and Race Differences by physical anthropologists and geneticists—June 1951

1. Scientists are generally agreed that all men living today belong to a single species, *Homo sapiens*, and are derived from a common stock, even though there is some dispute as to when and how different human groups diverged from this common stock.

The concept of race is unanimously regarded by anthropologists as a classificatory device providing a zoological frame within which the various groups of mankind may be arranged and by means of which studies of evolutionary processes can be facilitated. In its anthropological sense, the word "race" should be reserved for groups of mankind possessing well-developed and primarily heritable physical differences from other groups. Many populations can be so classified but, because of the complexity of human history, there are also many populations which cannot easily be fitted into a racial classification.

2. Some of the physical differences between human groups are due to differences in hereditary constitution and some to differences in the environ-

ments in which they have been brought up. In most cases, both influences have been at work. The science of genetics suggests that the hereditary differences among populations of a single species are the results of the action of two sets of processes. On the one hand, the genetic composition of isolated populations is constantly but gradually being altered by natural selection and by occasional changes (mutations) in the material particles (genes) which control heredity. Populations are also affected by fortuitous changes in gene frequency and by marriage customs. On the other hand, crossing is constantly breaking down the differentiations so set up. The new mixed populations, in so far as they, in turn, become isolated, are subject to the same processes, and these may lead to further changes. Existing races are merely the result, considered at a particular moment in time, of the total effect of such processes on the human species. The hereditary characters to be used in the classification of human groups, the limits of their variation within these groups, and thus the extent of the classificatory subdivisions adopted may legitimately differ according to the scientific purpose in view.

3. National, religious, geographical, linguistic and cultural groups do not necessarily coincide with racial groups; and the cultural traits of such groups have no demonstrated connexion with racial traits. Americans are not a race, nor are Frenchmen, nor Germans; nor *ipso facto* is any other national group. Muslims and Jews are no more races than are Roman Catholics and Protestants; nor are people who live in Iceland or Britain or India, or who speak English or any other language, or who are culturally Turkish or Chinese and the like, thereby describable as races. The use of the term "race" in speaking of such groups may be a serious error, but it is one which is habitually committed.

4. Human races can be, and have been, classified in different ways by different anthropologists. Most of them agree in classifying the greater part of existing mankind into at least three large units, which may be called major groups (in French *grand-races,* in German *Hauptrassen*). Such a classification does not depend on any single physical character, nor does, for example, skin colour by itself necessarily distinguish one major group from another. Furthermore, so far as it has been possible to analyse them, the differences in physical structure which distinguish one major group from another give no support to popular notions of any general "superiority" or "inferiority" which are sometimes implied in referring to these groups.

Broadly speaking, individuals belonging to different major groups of mankind are distinguishable by virtue of their physical characters, but individual members, or small groups, belonging to different races within the same major group are usually not so distinguishable. Even the major groups grade into each other, and the physical traits by which they and the races within them are characterized overlap considerably. With respect to most, if not all, measurable characters, the differences among individuals belonging to the same race are greater than the differences that occur between the observed averages for two or more races within the same major group.

5. Most anthropologists do not include mental characteristics in their classification of human races. Studies within a single race have shown that both innate capacity and environmental opportunity determine the results of tests of intelligence and temperament, though their relative importance is disputed.

When intelligence tests, even nonverbal, are made on a group of nonliterate people, their scores are usually lower than those of more civilized people. It has been recorded that different groups of the same race occupying similarly high levels of civilization may yield considerable differences in intelligence tests. When, however, the two groups have been brought up from childhood in similar environments, the differences are usually very slight. Moreover, there is good evidence that, given similar opportunities, the average performance (that is to say, the performance of the individual who is representative because he is surpassed by as many as he surpasses), and the variation round it, do not differ appreciably from one race to another.

Even those psychologists who claim to have found the greatest differences in intelligence between groups of different racial origin, and have contended that they are hereditary, always report that some members of the group of inferior performance surpass not merely the lowest ranking member of the superior group, but also the average of its members. In any case, it has never been possible to separate members of two groups on the basis of mental capacity, as they can often be separated on a basis of religion, skin colour, hair form or language. It is possible, though not proved, that some types of innate capacity for intellectual and emotional responses are commoner in one human group than in another, but it is certain that, within a single group, innate capacities vary as much as, if not more than, they do between different groups.

The study of the heredity of psychological characteristics is beset with difficulties. We know that certain mental diseases and defects are transmitted from one generation to the next, but we are less familiar with the part played by heredity in the mental life of normal individuals. The normal individual, irrespective of race, is essentially educable. It follows that his intellectual and moral life is largely conditioned by his training and by his physical and social environment.

It often happens that a national group may appear to be characterized by particular psychological attributes. The superficial view would be that this is due to race. Scientifically, however, we realize that any common psychological attribute is more likely to be due to a common historical and social background, and that such attributes may obscure the fact that, within different populations consisting of many human types, one will find approximately the same range of temperament and intelligence.

6. The scientific material available to us at present does not justify the conclusion that inherited genetic differences are a major factor in producing the differences between the cultures and cultural achievements of different peoples or groups. It does indicate, on the contrary, that a major factor in explaining such differences is the cultural experience which each group has undergone.

7. There is no evidence for the existence of so-called "pure" races. Skeletal remains provide the basis of our limited knowledge about earlier races. In regard to race mixture, the evidence points to the fact that human hybridization has been going on for an indefinite but considerable time. Indeed, one of the processes of race formation and race extinction or absorption is by means of hybridization between races. As there is no reliable evidence that disadvantageous effects are produced thereby, no biological justification exists for prohibiting inter-marriage between persons of different races.

8. We now have to consider the bearing of these statements on the problem of human equality. We wish to emphasize that equality of opportunity and equality in law in no way depend, as ethical principles, upon the assertion that human beings are in fact equal in endowment.

9. We have thought it worth while to set out in a formal manner what is at present scientifically established concerning individual and group differences.
(a) In matters of race, the only characteristics which anthropologists have so far been able to use effectively as a basis for classification are physical (anatomical and physiological).
(b) Available scientific knowledge provides no basis for believing that the groups of mankind differ in their innate capacity for intellectual and emotional development.
(c) Some biological differences between human beings within a single race may be as great as, or greater than, the same biological differences between races.
(d) Vast social changes have occurred that have not been connected in any way with changes in racial type. Historical and sociological studies thus support the view that genetic differences are of little significance in determining the social and cultural differences between different groups of men.
(e) There is no evidence that race mixture produces disadvantageous results from a biological point of view. The social results of race mixture, whether for good or ill, can generally be traced to social factors.

(Text drafted, at Unesco House, Paris, on 8 June 1951, by: Professor R. A. M. Bergman, Royal Tropical Institute, Amsterdam; Professor Gunnar Dahlberg, Director, State Institute for Human Genetics and Race Biology, University of Uppsala; Professor L. C. Dunn, Department of Zoology, Columbia University, New York; Professor J. B. S. Haldane, Head, Department of Biometry, University College, London; Professor M. F. Ashley Montagu,

NOTES

Chairman, Department of Anthropology, Rutgers University, New Brunswick, N.J.; Dr. A. E. Mourant, Director, Blood Group Reference Laboratory, Lister Institute, London; Professor Hans Nachtsheim, Director, Institut für Genetik, Freie Universität, Berlin; Dr. Eugène Schreider, Directeur adjoint du Laboratoire d'Anthropologie Physique de l'Ecole des Hautes Etudes, Paris; Professor Harry L. Shapiro, Chairman, Department of Anthropology, American Museum of Natural History, New York; Dr. J. C. Trevor, Faculty of Archaeology and Anthropology, University of Cambridge; Dr. Henri V. Vallois, Professeur au Museum d'Histoire Naturelle, Directeur du Musée de l'Homme, Paris; Professor S. Zuckerman, Head, Department of Anatomy, Medical School, University of Birmingham; Professor Th. Dobzhansky, Department of Zoology, Columbia University, New York, and Dr. Julian Huxley contributed to the final wording.)

3. More technical discussions of this subject will be found in: J. V. Neel and W. J. Schull, *Human Heredity*, Chicago, University of Chicago Press, 1954; C. Stern, *Human Genetics,* San Francisco, W. H. Freeman and Company, Publishers, 1960.

4. See G. W. Allport, *The Nature of Prejudice*, Cambridge, Mass., Addison-Wesley Publishing Company, Inc., 1954.

GENERAL REFERENCES

1. Origin of the Individual
BASIC INTRODUCTORY TEXTS IN MODERN BIOLOGY

Marsland, D. 1957. Principles of Modern Biology. New York: Henry Holt and Company, Inc.

Milne, L., and M. Milne. 1958. The Biotic World and Man. 2d ed. New York: Prentice-Hall, Inc.

Moore, J. 1957. Principles of Zoology. New York: Oxford University Press.

Simpson, G., C. Pittendrigh, and L. Tiffany. 1957. Life: An Introduction to Biology. New York: Harcourt, Brace and Company, Inc.

Weisz, P. 1959. The Science of Biology. New York: McGraw-Hill Book Company, Inc.

2. The Hereditary Information
BASIC INTRODUCTORY TEXTS IN GENETICS

Herskowitz, I. H. 1962. Genetics. Boston: Little, Brown and Company.

Sinnott, E. W., L. C. Dunn, and Th. Dobzhansky. 1958. Principles of Genetics. 5th ed. New York: McGraw-Hill Book Company, Inc.

Snyder, L. H., and P. R. David. 1957. The Principles of Heredity. 5th ed. Boston: D. C. Heath and Company.

Srb, A., and R. D. Owen. 1955. General Genetics. San Francisco: W. H. Freeman and Company, Publishers.

Stern, C. 1960. Principles of Human Genetics. 2d ed. San Francisco: W. H. Freeman and Company, Publishers.

3. Stability of the Hereditary Material

The textbooks of genetics listed for Chapter 2 contain accounts of mutability and chromosome changes and provide an introduction to the specialized literature. More general accounts of the genetic effects of radiation will be found in the following.

Auerbach, C. 1956. Genetics in the Atomic Age. New York: Essential Books.

Dobzhansky, Th., and B. Wallace. 1959. Radiation, Genes and Man. New York: Henry Holt and Company, Inc.

Effect of Radiation on Human Heredity. 1957. New York: World Health Organization.

Fowler, J. M. 1960. Fallout: A Study of Superbombs, Strontium 90 and Survival. New York: Basic Books, Inc.

Lapp, R. E., and J. Schubert. 1957. Radiation: What It Is and How It Affects You. New York: The Viking Press, Inc.

5. Heredity and Environment

Kallman, F. J. 1953. Heredity in Health and Mental Disorder. New York: W. W. Norton and Company, Inc.

Neel, J. V., and W. J. Schull. 1954. Human Heredity. Chicago: University of Chicago Press.

Newman, H. H. 1940. Multiple Human Births. New York: Doubleday, Doran and Company, Inc.

Newman, H. H., F. N. Freeman, and K. J. Holzinger. 1937. Twins: A Study of Heredity and Environment. Chicago: University of Chicago Press.

Penrose, L. S. 1961. Recent Advances in Human Genetics. Boston: Little, Brown and Company.

Stern, C. 1960. Principles of Human Genetics. 2d ed. San Francisco: W. H. Freeman and Company, Publishers.

Sutton, E. 1961. Genes, Enzymes and Inherited Diseases. New York: Holt, Rinehart and Winston, Inc.

7. Origin of the Human Species

Clark, W. E. L. 1955. The Fossil Evidence for Human Evolution. Chicago: University of Chicago Press.

GENERAL REFERENCES

―――― 1959. The Antecedents of Man. New York: Alfred A. Knopf, Inc.
Howells, W. 1959. Mankind in the Making. New York: Doubleday and Company, Inc.
Leakey, L. S. B. 1961. The Progress and Evolution of Man in Africa. New York: Oxford University Press.
Tax, S. 1960. The Evolution of Man. Vol. 2 of Evolution after Darwin. Chicago: University of Chicago Press.
Weidenreich, F. 1946. Apes, Giants and Man. Chicago: University of Chicago Press.

8. Evolutionary Forces as Applied to Man

Darwin, C. 1859. The Origin of Species. London.
Dobzhansky, Th. 1962. Mankind Evolving. New Haven: Yale University Press.
Dunn, L. C. 1959. Heredity and Evolution in Human Populations. Cambridge, Mass.: Harvard University Press.
Huxley, J. 1953. Evolution in Action. New York: Harper and Brothers.
Spuhler, J. N. 1958. Natural Selection in Man. Detroit: Wayne State University Press.

9. Isolation and Race Formation

Ashley Montagu, M. F. 1962. Culture and the Evolution of Man. New York: Oxford University Press.
Boyd, W. 1950. Genetics and the Races of Man. Boston: Little, Brown and Company.
Coon, C. S. 1948. The Races of Europe. New York: The Macmillan Company.
Coon, C. S., S. M. Garn, and J. B. Birdsell. 1950. Races. Springfield, Ill.: Charles C. Thomas, Publisher.
Dobzhansky, Th. 1962. Mankind Evolving. New Haven: Yale University Press.
Mourant, A. R. 1954. The Distribution of Human Blood Groups. Oxford: Blackwell Scientific Publications.

10. The Historic Breakdown of Isolation

Cook, R. C. 1951. Human Fertility, the Modern Dilemma. New York: William Sloane Associates, Inc.

Dunn, L. C., and Th. Dobzhansky. 1957. Heredity, Race and Society. New York: New American Library of World Literature, Inc.

Kroeber, A. L. 1952. The Nature of Culture. Chicago: University of Chicago Press.

—— 1953. Anthropology Today. Chicago: University of Chicago Press.

11. Heredity and Human Understanding

Comas, J. 1961. "Scientific" Racism Again? Current Anthropology 2: 303–40.

The Race Question in Modern Science. 1951. Paris: UNESCO.

INDEX

Albinism, 18, 21, 108-9, 112
American Indians, 151
Apes, 119-20
Artificial selection, 140-41, 156; in eugenics, 187-88
Australopithecines, 123-27, 204
Avery, O. T., 202

Biology, nature of, v
Blood groups, 43-44, 77; in one-egg twins, 82; in population groups, 106-8, 159
Brain, human, 80, 88-89, 94-96, 181; evolution of, 135, 144-48, 157, 162-63; see also Intelligence
Breeding, see Artificial Selection, Interbreeding
Broom, Robert, 204

Cancer, 48-50; of blood (leukemia), 53; of skin, 79
Carbon-14, 53
Cell, 2, 4, 9-11, Fig. 2, Fig. 3; death of, 36-39; impairment of, 42-43
Characters, hidden or "carried," 18, 20-21, 32, 109; multigenic nature of, 146, 187
Chase, M., 202
Chemical determiners, see Hereditary determinants
Chromosome, number in human, 11, 21, 57; "crossing over," 65-67; theory of heredity, 203

Chromosomes, 10, 12, Fig. 3, Fig. 4; paired condition of, 11, 16, 17, 19, 21, Fig. 7, 57-60, 69; abnormal number of, 39-40; infinite number of gene combinations in, 63-70; visible changes in, 36; see also Sex chromosomes
Complexity, in small objects, 3
Criminality, 86 (fig.) 94, 97, 180-81
Cultural inheritance, 145-46, 154-55, 161-62, 179; isolation in, 154-55, 169, 175
Culture, 125, 181, 195; Oldowan, 125; Chelles-Acheul, 128; of early man, 132-33, 146; and inborn mental capacities, 181-86; see also Cultural inheritance

Dart, Raymond, 204
Darwin, on origin of man, 119
Diabetes, 8, 25-26, 42-43, 78
Divergence, genetic, 113, 154, 190; cultural, 154-55, 173, 193
DNA, structure of, 28, 32, 202; synthesis of, 29, 202
Dobzhansky, Th., ix, 205
Dorn, H. F., 205
Dwarfism, 33-35; in sheep, 203

Egg, 2, 3, 5; fertilized, 1-3, 47; differences in, 6; formation of, 59-63, Fig. 1; see also Cells, Meiosis

Environment, as directive agent, 8, 9, 75-76, 160; interaction between optimal, and optimal heredity, 27; and heredity in intelligence, 97; see also Cultural inheritance
Ethics, lack of in nature, 137
Eugenics, 187-89
Evolution, as descent with change, 4, 110, 204; of man, 119-32, 146; blind alleys in, 130; speed in, 135-36, 143-44, 147; and natural selection, 136-39

Fallout, 50, 52-54
Feeblemindedness, mongolian idiocy, 39-40; within twins, 86 (fig.), 90-92; as handicap to cultural inheritance, 161-62; increase of with genetic variability, 176
Fertilization, 6, 69-70, 200, 201; see also Egg, Sperm
Filial generation, 18, 19
Fisher, R. A., 204
Florisbad man, 132
Fontéchevade man, 131

Genealogy, 100-1, 104
Gene frequency, in human populations, 108, 158-60, 162; forces which change it, 108-10, 118, 142, 162, 172-75
Gene pool, local, 106; sudivision of, 113, 143; racial, 152, 167; and species concept, 166-67; see also Inbreeding
Genes, 15; number of on one chromosome, 15, 63; dominant and recessive, 18, 20, 32, 111; chance and ratios in transmission of, 19-20, 61-71, 201; lethal and sublethal, 41-42; potential recombining ability of in egg and sperm, 63-70, 112; expression modified by environment, 75-79; see also Mutations, Hereditary determinants

Genetic health, of future generations, 47, 51; of present generations, 48, 53-55; see Cancer; see also Mutations
Genetics, aims of, 3, 8; and chemistry, 26; population, 108, 118, 204
Genius, see Intelligence
Genotype, 16-19, 101, 195

Haldane, J. B. S., 204
Hardy, G. H., 204
Heidelberg man, 130-31
Hemophilia, 35
Hereditary determinants, vii, 8, 15, 16, 30, 75; see also Genes
Hereditary material, effects of mitosis on, 11; nature of, 26-28, 31, 176; mutational changes in, 32-35; infinite combinations of genes in, 63-70, 112; environment and, 74-80; percentage of defects in, 186; see also Genes, Chromosome, Chromosomes, DNA, Twin studies
Heredity, interplay of, and environment, vii, 8-9, 27, 75-80, 158; as paradox of "similar but different," 7; hidden or "carried" characters in, 18, 20-21, 32, 109, 155-56; and DNA, 28; equal importance of all ancestors in, 101; see also Inheritance, Twin studies
Hershey, A. D., 202
Hertwig, Oscar, 200
Heterozygous, defined, 201
Homo sapiens, see Man
Homozygous, defined, 111, 201
Huntington's Chorea, 35
Huxley, J., 205
Hybrids, sterile, 167

Ice Age, see Pleistocene
Inbreeding, 105 (fig.), 111-13, 116, 173, 189-92
Inheritance, unique, of each person, vii, 2, 68, 70-71, 80, 100, 195; biological nature of, 1, 7, 8, 179;

INDEX

modified by environment, 9, 75-78; role of mitosis in, 11; of coat color in guinea pigs, 14, 16-19; equal role of sperm and egg in, 15; random nature of, 20, 45, 67-68, 162; *see also* Cultural inheritance

Intelligence, lack of broad differences within racial subgroups, viii, 160, 162-63, 176, 186, 192; relation of heredity and environment in, 84 (fig.), 92-93, 97; comparison of man's with other animals, 88-89, 96; tests, 89; head shape in relation to, 93 (fig.); genius level of, 93, 176; nature of, 95-96; in fossil ancestors of man, 145; relation of to cultures, 181-86

Intergroup tensions, vi, 196
Interracial crosses of man, 169, 192
Intersex, 24

Kanam man, 130-31
Kanjera man, 131
Kettlewell, H., 204
Kornberg, A., 202

Leakey, L. S. B., discoveries of in Tanganyika, 127, 204
Leukemia, 53
Life, origin of, 1, 4-5; as "force," 4; Pasteur on, 199-200
Living substance, 3-4, 25; abilities of, 9, 24; importance of proteins in, 25; *see also* Cell

McCarty, M., 202
MacLeod, C. M., 202
Mammalia, 120
Man, geographical origin of, viii, 119, 148; fossil ancestors of, 121-32; relationship of modern to ancestors, 125-26; hybridization among ancestors of, 132; origin of in time, 132-33, 170; common ancestry of modern, 133, 167-70

Meiosis, 59-61
Mendel, Gregor, 14, 201
Mentality, *see* Intelligence, Feeblemindedness
Mental retardation, *see* Feeblemindedness
Metabolism, 42-43
Migrations, of man, 150; and breakdown of isolates, 173-74, 191
Miller, Stanley, 200
Mitosis, 10-12, Fig. 3
Mongolian idiocy, 40, 90
Monkeys, 120
Mount Carmel man, 132
Muller, H. J., 203
Multiracial society, 191
Muscular dystrophy, 35, 41
Mutations, 31-44, 53, 136, 141; rates in, 35; harmful nature of most, 35-43, 46-48; with slight effects, 42; causes of, 44-47; random nature of, 45-46, 136, 140, 144; as carried along during gene recombination, 70

Natural selection, 136-39, 143-44; in moths in England, 138-39; as operating in man, 155-57
"Nature and nurture," 75, 180-82; *see also* Environment, Heredity
Neanderthal man, 129, 130
Nucleus, 2-3; division of, 10-11, Fig. 3, 200; *see also* Cell

Oreopithecus fossil, 122-23
Outbreeding, 110, 114-16, 190-92

Paleontology, nature of, 118-20
Paranthropus, 126
Parthenogenesis, 200
Pasteur, Louis, 199
Peking man, *see* Pithecanthropines
Phenotype, 17
Phenylketonuria, 90
Pincus, G., 200
Pithecanthropines, 127-30

Pleistocene, evolution of man in, 124-30
Population explosion, 175-76
Population genetics, *see* Gene frequency
Populations, genetic nature of, 109; semi-isolated units in, 110-15, 143, 153-54, 192-93, 195-96; breakdown of isolates in, 172-73; recombinational, 191; *see also* Races of man
Primates, 121
Proconsul fossils, 121-22
Proteins, in living material, 4, 25; primordial development of, 5, 200; types of, blood, 43-44
Pygmy tribes, 154

Race, concept of, 151
Races of man, early formation of, viii, 150-51; subgrouping in, 151-54; role of natural selection in, 155-57; group differences within, 158-60
Radiation, damage, 36-40, 45-48, 50-54, 188; types of, 45, 47, 51
Random drift, 156-57
Recessive genes, as lethal and sublethal, 41-42; and inbreeding, 189
RH genes, 44, 90
Rhodesian man, *see* Pithecanthropines
Rickets, 87-88

Schizophrenia, 86 (fig.), 91, 161
Sex, equal role of each in heredity, 15, 58; chromosomes, 21-22; mode of determination of in cell at fertilization, 21-24
Sex chromosomes, 21-24, 57, Fig. 4, 201-2
Sheppard, P. M., 205
Sibs, 84
Simpson, G. G., 204
Skin color, 76

Solo man, 127
Specialization, rarely reversed in evolution, 126
Species, nature of, 166-68; concept in man, 168-70
Sperm, 2, 3, 5, 6; equal in potency in inheritance, 7; formation of, 59-61, Fig. 1; *see also* Egg, fertilized, Meiosis, Cell
Staining, 10
Stebbins, G. L., Jr., 205
Steinheim man, 130-31
Sterility, 24; between species, 167-68
Strontium-90, 52-54
Sutton, Walter, 203
Swanscombe man, 131

Ternafine man, 130-31
Tools, primitive, 125, 127-29
Trinil man, 127
Tuberculosis, 85-87
Twins, identical, 11, 81; twin studies, 81-94
Two-egg twins, 82; compared with one-egg, 83-92

UNESCO committee statement on race, 205-9

Variability, genetic, 112, 114-15, 141, 143-44, 171, 175; in racial subgroups, 152, 154-57; confusion between, in individual, and in group, 158, 179; *see also* Hereditary material, Inbreeding, Divergence

Watson-Crick model, 202
Weinberg, W., 203
Wright, S., 204, 205

Yolk, 6

Zinjanthropus, *see* Australopithecines